Rosson

Outlaws in Petticoats

and Other Notorious Texas Women

Ann Ruff and Gail Drago

Republic of Texas Press
an imprint of
Wordware Publishing, Inc.

Library of Congress Cataloging-in-Publication Data

Ruff, Ann, 1930-1993.
    Outlaws in petticoats and other notorious Texas women / by Ann
    Ruff and Gail Drago.
        p.   cm. — (Women of the West series)
    Includes bibliographical references and index.
    ISBN 1-55622-315-3
    1. Women—Texas—Biography. 2. Texas—Biography. I. Texas—
    History. I. Drago, Gail, 1947- . II. Title. III. Title: Outlaws in
    petticoats. IV. Series: Women of the West series
    (Plano, Tex.)
    CT262.R82   1994
    920.72'09764--dc20
    [B]   94-45381
                                   CIP

ISBN 1-55622-315-3
10 9 8 7 6 5 4 3 2 1
9412

All inquiries for volume purchases of this book should be addressed to
Wordware Publishing, Inc., at the above address. Telephone inquiries may be
made by calling:

(214) 423-0090

Dedication

Remember

Ann Ruff

1930—1993

She rode off into the sunset.

Photo courtesy of Richard Wright and Martha Berryman.

Women of the West
a series from Republic of Texas Press

Women of the West brings readers fascinating stories about the women who helped shape the West as we know it. From the early Native American to contemporary women, this series strives to identify all women of the West through compelling accounts of the relationships, character, and determination that enabled women not only to survive but in many cases triumph with grace and dignity over difficult, even seemingly impossible, circumstances.

The series presents stories of daring and legendary women as well as those of quiet strength and subtle persuasion. Not all were good, nor did they always make the right choices. Some women were driven by greed, desperation, and even revenge, and those dark sides are also revealed.

The **Women of the West** series is rich with a heritage of the unusual, extraordinary women whose experiences, far from exaggerated, have become today's legends.

Mary Elizabeth Goldman, Editor

Contents

Introduction

From the pages of *Outlaws in Petticoats*, thirteen enigmatic women ride again out of a diverse past to tickle our interest in the unconventional. Their stories are provocative ones which challenge our sensitivities and intrigue us with plots and subplots so typical of the nonconformist. Historians and folklorists sometime differ in their assessment of these characters, but they agree that their lives add brilliance to the already vivid history of the Lone Star State.

Perhaps this sorority of soul mates were the true children of an untamed Texas, known for mothering a restless breed. In many ways, these women shared the same virtues and vices as the land itself, for until this century, Texas was wild, yet beautiful—a virgin territory struggling for its own identity. In comparison, eight of these individuals were hauntingly lovely, a trait they skillfully used to their advantage. Unlike that maiden land, however, none depicted here could testify to being virgin. With the exception of four who devoted their lives to only one man, the remaining nine shared marriages and romantic interludes with a total of over fifty men. The sheer number is testimony to the fact that they were not very wise in the affairs of the heart, as they also had an uncanny knack for choosing the wrong man. A couple even paid for their mistakes with their lives, such as the tenacious Sally Skull, who may have killed one husband only to die at the hands of another. As for Bonnie Parker, who allowed her man to place her in the path of danger, her blood mingled with Clyde's in a final fateful moment on a dusty Louisiana farm road.

Another thread, that of nonconformity, connects these women, whose lifetimes span from the Texas Revolution to the New Deal. From outlaw Belle Starr, to entrepreneur, Lizzie Johnson Williams, to camp follower Sarah Bourjett, most shared a burning desire to rise above their male counterparts. But curiously, masculine approval in their business dealings as well as in their personal lives stood as a priority. They also thrived on change. With early Texas politics in constant turmoil, these women remained dynamic, changing like a chameleon to fit the evolving world around them. While nineteenth-century society maintained as gospel the status quo, these lawless spirits carved out their own set of rules. To describe them as a colorful clan is indeed an understatement. Formidable figures who stood in the shadows of morality, they refused to be imprisoned by a narrow code of conduct and remained stout-hearted mistresses of their own souls. As a result, they suffered "the slings and arrows" sent by gossips.

The hard fact was that the majority of these characters, which included gamblers, paramours, horse traders, outlaws, prostitutes, and political pioneers tolerated the law until it blocked their way. Then, they stepped lightly and quietly around it. Remorse was an emotion not well understood by them, as seemed to be the case with the "Confederate Paul Revere," Sophia Porter, who caused the violent death of one of her "best" husbands. Many others, such as the stunning Harriet Potter Ames and the mysterious Adah Isaacs Menken, often found themselves before a judge fending off accusations. They always felt perfectly justified in their beliefs.

Obviously, none of the thirteen here could stand as paragons whose histories remain flawless under careful examination. They were, in contrast, fearless females who questioned the Victorian stereotypical woman, depicted as standing on the proverbial verandah waiting for her soldier to come riding through the cotton fields. For crack shots like Skull and Starr, the proper rules of etiquette made perfect target practice. As for role reversal, Sarah Bowman never gave it a thought when she marched out onto the battlefield to rescue "her boys" who lay wounded and dying. Neither did

Lizzie Johnson Williams, who raised eyebrows when she climbed stockyard fences to bargain for prime head.

Once the smoke of the Victorian century cleared, these outlaws in petticoats and lawless in spirit seemed the quintessence of human strength—the driving force that settled a brutal land. Though they were not the virtuous type, their lives speak volumes about the hardy Texas female who always stood ready to defend her ground in a hot, harsh frontier. But what of this century that found itself moving ahead, aboard Henry Ford's marvelous mobile machine? Other Texas women of dubious decision-making skills also made the papers. While Bonnie was terrorizing a five-state territory with her true love, Clyde, Governor Miriam Ferguson was pulling the hoods of the Ku Klux Klan, all the while engaging in unconventional political maneuvers. Also true to her man, "Ma" Ferguson rattled critics' cages by trying to reinstate her impeached predecessor and husband, Jim Ferguson.

The world of fashion didn't quite fit the needs of these women either. Most were ornate dressers who shared a fetish for feathers, fringe, and flamboyance. Belle Starr went in for the shock effect. When she wasn't dressed in buckskin and fringe as she raced her horse Venus down the Dallas streets, she was prancing through a hotel lobby in a velvet dress accented with pearl-handled six-shooters and a plumed Stetson hat. Harriet Potter Ames, who married the enigmatic Robert Potter, Secretary of the Texas Navy, designed everything from her Grecian-styled wedding gown to a riding habit inspired by the Caddo Indians. The unlucky Diamond Bessie gave up her life rather than her jewels which she traditionally wore day and night. The flash of these women yielded new meaning to the phrase "fashion statement," and in doing so became either the rage or a ridicule among their peers.

When doing research for this book, one problem surfaced with almost every subject. The line between fact and fiction was so dim that some of the women appeared to have more than one face. In some cases, the dilemma could be traced back to the subjects themselves, for they loved to shroud themselves in mystery. In fact, they perpetuated their own myths by fabricating tales about their pasts that could never be verified. The result is a collection of contradictions, particularly about Sophia Porter and Adah Menken. Sophia romanticized that she was the first female to set foot on the San Jacinto Battlefield after the last shot was fired. And, when asked by newspaper reporters where she was born, actress Adah Isaacs Menken rotated among five exotic birthplaces, yet never mentioned the true one—Nacogdoches, Texas.

In other cases, the battle between truth and tall tale is traced to the lack of recorded histories. Whether some of these women were victors or victims varies from one account to another. Such is the case of the beautiful Emily Morgan, a famous "Yellow Rose" slave victimized by Santa Anna. Some reports portray Emily as smarter than she was given credit for being. She may have just turned the tables on her own captor and thus brought about the Texas win at San Jacinto. If it hadn't been for her, report some, the amorous Mexican general would have never been caught "with his pants down." Four decades later, Bessie Rothschild also became a victim, murdered by her husband, Abe Rothschild. And in Bessie's case, as well, vengeance may have been hers, as the prominent Rothschild name was forever marred by trial publicity.

Shakespeare would have found much material in these complex characters, certainly all victims of their own tragic flaws. From the wrath of Belle Starr to the pride of Sophia Porter to the passion of Bonnie Parker, they paid for their sins, yet lived life by their own rules. These spirited outlaws were indeed entrepreneurs—in the business of promoting their own destinies. Whether history chooses to remember them as shady characters who could challenge the devil himself or as women who gave something worth keeping to their era remains to be seen. What matters is that they were powerful forerunners to a time when women are looked upon as equals. Obviously, they chose the "road less taken." No doubt they traveled it in style.

HARRIET MOORE PAGE POTTER AMES

Heroine of a Thousand Tales

1807-1890

Harriet looked out over the ancient cypress trees that cast long dark shadows across the glassy water of Caddo Lake. The sun's rays, painting the evening canvas sky with pinks, golds, and purples, now fanned themselves behind gossamer clouds. Warm and safe within her bear robe as she stood beside her new husband, she couldn't be happier. As far as Harriet could see and in every direction, the land was theirs—hers and Rob's. Potter's Point was now legally their own piece of heaven—acreage acquired for her husband's contribution to the newly formed Republic of Texas.

How could Harriet have known that Rob had recently written a will leaving their land to his mistress? While she had kept Potter's Point in operation, Rob, past Secretary of the Texas Navy and newly elected senator, had been spending all his leisure time in Austin with a married woman. A man of eloquent language, he had tricked Harriet into believing that she was the only woman for him. She should have recognized his flaws, though he kept them concealed under a formally correct demeanor. He was like Solomon Page, her first husband, too afraid of making a commitment to give himself wholly to another human being. And like Solomon, he, too, was a dashing and handsome man, but then all of Harriet's husbands were dashing and handsome. Even though she was known as "one of the bravest women in Texas," heroic Harriet wasn't always wise in affairs of the heart.

Solomon Page came into her life when she was seventeen years old—the perfect age to be easily impressed with good looks, expensive clothes, and a mysterious past. She met Solomon when he called on her father, Dr. Francis Moore, as a patient. Solomon had only suffered a very minor injury to his hand, but he was extremely nervous and agitated. His small wound assumed major proportions and Harriet naively thought the object of her infatuation must be a talented musician. After the young man's third visit to Dr. Moore, it was obvious his hand was no longer his main concern. As he departed, he took Harriet's hands in his and said, "You are the woman I need. I will return for you."

Harriet was truly dazzled. If ever a young girl was in love, it was Harriet Ann Moore with Solomon Page. She sat down to wait for her lover to come for her, confident of his love. And, she waited and waited and waited. An older woman might have figured out that something was amiss, but "waiting for Solomon" was to become the recurring refrain of Harriet's life with him.

At last her lover returned. He brought presents for everyone, none of them appropriate. For Dr. Moore who didn't smoke, the gift was tobacco; a scarlet bag for Mrs. Moore who loathed red; and sweets for Harriet in a flavor she hated. Later in life Harriet would learn how much the true nature of a man is exposed with the presents he bestows on women.

Totally blind to her fiancee's faults, Harriet married Solomon in Dr. Moore's home. The honeymoon was postponed until after they settled in the house that Solomon had acquired. He had not bothered to have it cleaned, so the new bride became the cleaning lady. It seems strange, but no one, not even Harriet's father, knew what Solomon did for a living. Solomon had murmured something vague about buying and selling goods. In an age of strict parental approval, Dr. Moore seems to have entirely ignored his new son-in-law's source of income. Harriet and her stepmother were always at odds, and perhaps Dr. Moore saw his daughter's marriage as the answer to a calmer existence.

Harriet almost immediately found herself spending entire evenings alone waiting for Solomon. In her innocence, she imagined every sort of disaster befalling him, but he always returned. She was never sure where he had been, nor would he tell her. One day Solomon asked her to loan him her wedding ring. He would only need it a few days, and it would be returned. Business had been bad, and the ring was needed for security. As a dutiful wife, Harriet pulled it from her finger. True, the ring was returned to her hand, but a week later it was gone again. Harriet was totally unable to refuse her husband's requests, and she was too proud to ask for her father's help.

Harriet's family decided to leave Tennessee and try their fortune in Texas, and before he left, Dr. Moore gave her $100 and the admonition she was to go to her grandmother in Kentucky if she were ever in distress. Finally growing suspicious of her husband's business dealings, she had the sense to hide the $100 and not tell Solomon about the gift, at least for a while.

The weeks went by, and Solomon became more nervous and irritable every day. He began asking her if she had any money, and Harriet foolishly told him about the $100. He pleaded with her for it, and she refused. He argued and then he wept. She wept, too, but still refused him the money. Finally, Solomon confessed, "It's a gambling debt, Hatty. A gambling debt." Solomon's "business" was finally exposed.

Harriet remained resolute. "It's my money, Solomon." she said, "Reliance money. You have given me no money; I have been too timid to ask for any. I have been wanting to ask you for some money to buy baby clothes, but—" Solomon was livid! "Not that, too, Hatty!" The last thing the gambler wanted was the responsibility of a baby.

That night, as Harriet pretended to sleep, Solomon searched the house for the $100. As she listened to his prowling, the girl began to honestly evaluate her marriage for the first time. Solomon was a gambler, but she loved him, and she was committed to a man who would never accept responsibility. Finally, when she agreed to give him $50, he changed immediately to a kind and devoted husband, but she knew in her heart it would soon be the old scene again of "waiting for Solomon."

Then Solomon got lucky. The man to whom he was heavily in debt was murdered, and all records were burned. The gambler proclaimed this was an omen of good luck, and as Harriet had feared, he returned to his addiction. Even the birth of his son, Joseph, did not keep this dedicated card shark from the tables. One night, Solomon came home excited. They were moving to New Orleans. Before she had a chance to object, he sold the house without her knowledge, and she had no choice but to climb on the coach for Louisiana. Women of Harriet's time were so totally dependent upon men, it probably never occurred to Harriet to remain in Tennessee and survive on her own. It was her duty to go with her husband.

In 1830 Harriet and Solomon settled down to a life of living on the edge. Harriet never knew when Solomon would come home broke, but gambling was all he ever wanted to do. He had no concept of earning an honest living. Even after their second child, little Ginny, was born, Solomon totally ignored his children. He never bought them gifts, played with them, or noticed them. While Harriet dreamed of a loving marriage and family, Solomon yearned only for a great fortune to be made on a lucky draw of the cards. And, even when Harriet was deathly ill with yellow fever, Solomon never showed a moment's concern.

Determined to make the best of the situation, Harriet opened up her own boutique, where she sold ladies clothes and notions. She was quite good at designing and sewing the latest fashions in dresses and hats. Before long, Harriet's business prowess began to pay off. With her talent for style and her beauty, Harriet's shop became a great success. Just as she was feeling good about her accomplishments, Solomon came in with another surprise. "Hatty, we're going to Texas!" he exclaimed as he looked at her for the first time in weeks. Solomon painted a glowing picture of how life would be in Texas. With free land, he would work hard, and soon they would be living on a great plantation. Harriet didn't believe that for one minute, but she did want to be near her family again. "I'll go with you to Texas, Solomon," she agreed. But she knew it would be her money that would take them there. As usual, Solomon was broke and in debt, and Harriet would never have another little shop again.

The Page family landed at Velasco sometime in the spring of 1835. Harriet's brother, John, met them and took his sister to visit her father who had settled along Chocolate Bayou near Galveston. Solomon was left behind to follow the next day with the household goods. Harriet should have known better than to ever leave Solomon alone. He did follow the next day, but the wagon was empty except for a barrel of flour. Solomon Page had spent his first day in Texas gambling. All of Harriet's possessions and money were gone. John was so furious with his brother-in-law he wanted to kill him, and he hated Solomon the rest of his life.

Solomon and Harriet spent the summer with Harriet's father and her stepmother. The Moore's contempt of Solomon was so obvious, he finally left. Where he got the money, no one knew, but he soon returned with a few supplies for his family and moved them to a desolate cabin in the wilderness several miles out of Velasco. Harriet had enough food for three days when Solomon left to see about a nearby job. He was to bring supplies back to them. Once again Harriet waited for her husband, but this time waiting was a matter of life and death. The three days passed and more days. She and the children began to starve. She managed to find some ripened berries, the only food that kept them alive. Finally, on the sixth day Solomon arrived on horseback, but he did not bring food or supplies of any kind. Harriet went wild with fury. Unable to understand why Harriet was so angry, Solomon revealed he had enlisted in the Texas army. Then, why had he bothered to return at all? Why not just leave them to die, she screamed. Suddenly, she realized it was for her money. But hunger and desertion had made Harriet strong. She vowed she would throw her savings in the bayou before she gave Solomon a cent.

The next morning the gambler mounted his horse and calmly rode off, leaving his family without provisions to exist or livestock for transportation. Somehow, with incredible courage, Harriet kept them alive. Her hatred of Solomon knew no bounds. At times she thought she was losing her mind with hunger and grief, but she survived. Help came at last with a passing traveler, and she returned to the safety of her father's home a sadder but wiser woman where Solomon Page was concerned.

In the meantime, big events were taking place in Texas. Poor Harriet had no idea, or cared, what was going on. Neither Sam Houston, the Alamo, nor Santa Anna had any meaning. All she wanted was food and safety for her family. John, her brother, had gone off to war with the promise to return. His wife, Amy, and Harriet shared a small cabin, and from Amy, Harriet learned to be a true farm girl. She learned to plant a garden, milk the cow, tend the livestock, and hundreds of other chores expected of a pioneer woman. Harriet discovered she was happy for the first time since Solomon brought her to Texas.

When the Alamo fell to the Mexican army, word of the disaster spread; terrified Texans began to flee from the troops of the mighty Santa Anna. Amy's parents arrived in a wagon and forced their daughter to go with them in spite of her pleas to be allowed to wait for John. Harriet, young Joe, and baby Ginny were alone again, but this time they knew better than to wait for Solomon.

To overcome her loneliness for Amy's company, one day Harriet dressed herself and the children in all their finery and set out to meet people in town. But the people were running out to meet her. How strange, Harriet thought. Where are they going? Then she began to hear the gunfire in the distance. Horses and loaded wagons were frantically rushing past her. Somehow she got the children on a wagon and trudged along behind through the mud. Harriet had no idea where they were going and was even a bit vague on who they were running from, but she did know the Page family were the best-dressed group in the Runaway Scrape!

When the wagons halted, Harriet found herself and the children abandoned. The farm women in their calico and sunbonnets instantly distrusted a woman in a dress *above the ankles* and refused to take the Page family with them. Then, fate intervened in Harriet's life again. Two men rode up to the camp. Harriet immediately recognized Colonel Hall, a friend of her father's. Would he help her? The gallant colonel was delighted to be of aid to his old friends.

With Colonel Hall was a handsome man with black hair that shone in the sun and dressed in uniform. His boots were highly polished, and when he spoke, his voice was that of an educated gentleman. Harriet was introduced to Colonel Robert E. Potter, Secretary of the Texas Navy. One very important asset Harriet possessed other than bravery was beauty. Robert Potter took one look at her and fell in love. Harriet was immediately placed under his protection, and she and her children would be escorted safely to Velasco. Ginny and Joe rode behind Potter's slave, and Harriet was gently lifted to Colonel Potter's horse to ride behind him. Here was a romantic rescue right out of a storybook. Rob Potter was her handsome prince, and she was his fairy princess. Harriet should have known better.

Robert Potter was a man of many personalities. He had served in the U.S. Navy as a midshipman for six years. Then he studied law and was elected to the North Carolina House of Commons. Immediately upon his arrival to Texas, the people of Nacogdoches had elected him to serve at the Convention for Independence held at Washington-on-the-Brazos. Potter signed the Declaration of Independence and was appointed Secretary of the Texas Navy. For his services to Texas he expected to receive a large parcel of land in northeast Texas.

But there was a dark side to Potter's nature. Slaves called it the "mark of Satan." What he neglected to tell Harriet was that in 1831, in an extreme fit of jealous rage, he had accused his former wife of adultery with her cousin and her minister. In a black rage of revenge, he attacked both men with a knife and castrated them. Potter saw himself as the justified avenger but was sentenced to jail for two years. His wife, innocent of adultery, divorced him.

When he was released from jail, Potter ran for the House of Commons and won. Even though he had committed a heinous crime, he was still able to charm the voters. But Potter's sick and consuming temper was to get the best of him. He was expelled from the House for "playing a game of cards unfairly." Not only did Rob Potter have a raging, vicious temper, he cheated at cards. Insulted, he left for Texas, but the stories of his proficiency with a knife followed him with the term "Potterizing."

Harriet knew nothing of her rescuer's past. All she cared about was that he was extremely kind to her and her children. Potter gave them refuge aboard his ship, the *Flash*, and it was just a matter of days before Rob Potter was professing his undying love for her. He was thirty-six years old, ten years older than Harriet, but how different he was from the ne're-do-well gambler, Solomon Page! Here was a man with ambition, talent, education, and a brilliant mind. Even though she hated Solomon and returned Rob Potter's love, Harriet was married and refused to get a divorce. In those days, divorce was not looked upon lightly, unless your husband went around castrating innocent men. Harriet believed her only alternative was to go to her grandmother's home in Kentucky.

While still on Potter's ship, Harriet's beloved daughter, Ginny, became deathly ill with a fever. Overtaken with grief, Harriet blamed Page over and over for bringing them to Texas and causing her little girl's illness. As she watched the life ebb out of the child, Potter arrived with the news that Solomon Page had been killed. Harriet felt nothing for the man who had brought her unbearable grief. All she could do was mourn the loss of her precious daughter.

Harriet and young Joe remained aboard ship with Potter while the gossip flew about their relationship. Harriet ignored the tales; she was still obsessed with the loss of Ginny. One day, as Harriet sat in Rob's cabin mending his clothes, a man came to the door. He was thin, filthy, and smelled of whiskey. Harriet stared as recognition finally dawned. Solomon Page was not dead. He was here! As the wretch began to talk, Harriet sat in shock. Amazingly, he had come to get her and the children. Solomon told her he would forgive her relationship with Potter, just come back to him. Harriet was furious! The death of Ginny, Solomon's desertion of his family in the wilderness, their near starvation, and his gambling were too much for Harriet. Her anger knew no bounds, and the two insulted each other with consuming hatred. When Solomon staggered from the cabin, it was the last time she would ever see him.

After the war was over, Rob Potter went to claim his headright in the dark piney woods of East Texas. He begged Harriet to come with him, but she refused. She was still married, and she would have to go to her grandmother's in Kentucky. On the pretense of escorting his beloved part way to Kentucky, Potter instead took her into East Texas to the land awarded him for his service to the Republic, Potter's Point. And, she had to stay with him until a party traveling east could take her to Kentucky.

Rob wooed Harriet with an ardor that swept her off her feet. He declared his love for her and said she must stay with him forever. Flowers, poetry, and even his violin praised the beauty of sweet Harriet. Still, Harriet felt she must return east, no matter how badly she wanted to stay with Rob. She was married, and Solomon Page was far from dead.

The silver tongued Potter did not give up his quest. One day, he asked Harriet about her marriage. Was it a Catholic union? Of course it wasn't. She and Solomon were married at her home in Tennessee. Then Potter asked if she had remarried in the Catholic Church when she came to Texas? No. Well, then, the wily Potter pointed out, she really wasn't married at all. Texas belonged to Mexico when the Pages came to Velasco, and according to Mexican law, all emigrants had to be married in the Catholic Church. Actually, when Stephen F. Austin received his grant from Mexico, the Mexican government required Catholicism as the religion for settlers, but very few Texans obeyed the law. Even though Harriet and Solomon were not remarried under Mexican law, Joe was their legitimate child because he was born in the United States before they came to Texas. She should have seen it as a lawyer's ploy.

Harriet was skeptical of all these confusing laws, but Potter finally convinced her he was absolutely right. After all, she thought, he is a lawyer, and it is his business to know these things. Harriet finally accepted Potter's arguments. Though intelligent about many things, she accepted Potter's easy cancellation of her marriage to Solomon Page without a legal divorce. Harriet even foolishly agreed to Potter's proposal to marry by bond, rather than a civil or religious ceremony. They would sign a statement, properly witnessed, that they were married. Since no clergymen or judges were in the wilderness, Potter said this bond would be legally binding. Happiness seemed so easy to Harriet. So, on September 5, 1836, Rob and Harriet signed a bond of marriage with the statement, "It is our honest intent and purpose to consider this ceremony as a permanent and binding state of wedlock."

Life was bliss for Mrs. Robert Potter. The land that surrounded the dark, murky Caddo Lake was theirs. She loved the land, she loved her life with Rob, and she was going to have a baby. But Potter's lurid past finally found its way to the woods of East Texas and to Harriet. One day Rob took his wife for a visit to their closest neighbors. While Rob was visiting with the husband, the wife told Harriet the gory castration story. Harriet listened with a stoic countenance. She would never show any of the turmoil she felt. In addition to the mutilation of two men, Rob had lied and told her he had never married. Not only had he been married, he had two children. Harriet could not wait to get away from the gossiping woman. As they returned home, Harriet confronted her husband with his past. She wanted the truth. He seemed almost relieved that she knew, and of course, Harriet forgave him.

Potter was away from home when his son was born dead. Luckily, an acquaintance of Potter's came by and helped Harriet in her distress. He was Charles Ames. One look at Harriet and Charles was head over heels in love. No one would ever know his deep feelings for the beautiful woman who had turned to him in her hour of need. Charles Ames was a totally honest man, loyal to his friends, a hard worker, and he helped his fellow man. Of all the qualities to admire in a man, they could be found in Charles Ames.

Rob was seldom at Potter's Point. His ambition and desire for political power had returned, and he was elected senator to the Congress of the Republic of Texas. Letters to his beloved Harriet from Austin arrived often with news of the legislature and the political scene. As for his social life in the capital, Potter had very few comments. And, in spite of Harriet's urging, Potter kept putting off recording their bond of marriage.

Solomon Page finally sued Harriet for divorce. She questioned Potter as to why Page acquired a divorce when, according to Potter, she and Solomon were not legally married in Mexico or Texas. Why was a divorce even necessary? Potter quieted her with some legal mumbo jumbo and assured her that she was legally Mrs. Robert Potter. As for recording their bond, he would get to it—someday. More children were born to Harriet and Rob. Life was fairly serene, and Harriet became the perfect pioneer wife. She never complained of hard work or loneliness while her husband was in Austin. Charles Ames made an occasional appearance on a visit, and Harriet was always delighted to see him.

Trouble was brewing in East Texas, and, naturally, Rob Potter was in the middle of the ruckus of the Regulator-Moderator War between 1839 and 1844. Rather than a war, it was more of a feud. Each group wanted to take over running the territory, and a reign of terror resulted. Men were ambushed, prisoners were hanged without trial, and many families were driven from their homes. Violence was so intense, Sam Houston arrived to settle the trouble. In August of 1844, both sides agreed to peace, but it was too late to save Rob Potter's life.

Potter took the side of the Moderators, and he had made a hated enemy of the Regulator leader, William P. Rose. On March 2, 1842, a group of armed men led by Rose surrounded Harriet's home on Potter's Point. Harriet feared certain death, but she prepared to fight. Rob peered through a crack in the wall and observed very calmly, "There are too many, Hatty, too many. I'll make a run for it to the lake. If I can make the lake, I'll be safe. It is my life they want, not yours."

Harriet and the children begged for him to stay inside. They pleaded and wept, but Rob was determined. Rose wanted him dead, and if he stayed, his family would be killed, too. With probably the only decent gesture of his life, Rob flung open the cabin door and ran like the wind. Shots were fired all around him, but miraculously he reached the lake unhurt. Then Potter did a strange thing. He paused and carefully propped his loaded gun on a tree before diving into the water. One of the gang fired at Rob in the lake but missed. Then, the Regulator rushed up and grabbed the fleeing man's loaded gun he had left by the tree. When Rob came up for air, the son-in-law of old Rose took careful aim and fired. Robert Potter died instantly. His death was the finest moment in his life. At least he saved his family. A storm washed his body ashore the next day, and Harriet buried him at Potter's Point.

Harriet bravely insisted on prosecuting Rob's murderers. She left her home and children and fought endless futile battles to see that the murderers were punished. As she was about to see the end of Rose and his gang, a disaster befell

Harriet that would last throughout her life and years after her death. Robert Potter's will arrived. He had left the bulk of his land to a special friend, Mrs. Sophia Ann Mayfield of Austin, wife of Colonel James S. Mayfield, a member of the Congress. Potter even bequeathed his favorite horse to Colonel Mayfield. But, the worst blow of all was that in his will he referred to Harriet as "Mrs. Harriet A. Page," not "Mrs. Harriet Potter." Harriet received only a small portion of Potter's Point, and nothing at all was left to his children.

The will was the final blow to her case against Rose and his gang. As Harriet Page, Robert Potter's wife only by bond, her testimony would have no validity. She had to be recognized as Robert Potter's legal widow. Harriet had no choice but to return home, and Rob's murderers were set free. More sorrow awaited Harriet. Her little baby girl, Lakeann, was scalded to death when a tub of boiling lye soap overturned on the child. Harriet was wild with grief. It was too much for anyone to bear. As she cried her heart out over her baby's grave, Charles Ames returned to her life to comfort her and save her sanity.

Epilogue: Harriet married Charles Ames and had twelve more children. She died in the home of her son, Edward Yancy Ames, in New Orleans. A legal battle over possession of Potter's Point lasted for years between the Ames and the Mayfield heirs. The courts refused to accept the legality of Harriet and Rob's marriage, and in 1875 Chief Justice Oran M. Roberts upheld Potter's will as it had been written. As historian Dr. Fred Tarpley comments, "Thus concluded Harriet's life in Texas; a sad portrait of nineteenth-century woman's absolute legal and social dependence upon her man."

SARAH BOURJETT BOWMAN

The Great Western

1812, 1813, or 1817-1866

A soldier once called her a Joan of Arc. Sylvester Mowry, a lusty frontiersman, wrote that she was "an admirable pimp." The army labeled her a hero. The Indians feared her. She was supernatural, they thought. But no sobriquet better fits Sarah Bourjett than "The Great Western," a fallen angel *extraordinaire* who was a mother and a madam, a camp follower and a cook, a heroine and a healer. She ran hospitals, bawdy houses, mess halls, and her own private orphanage and still had time to test the romantic waters over and over and over. Immortalized in the many memoirs of soldiers who knew her, The Great Western filled all needs of "her boys," and, in the process, helped the United States forge its movement westward.

Sarah made her grand entrance into the United States Army via the Mexican War. In 1845 President James Polk was concerned with proposed annexation of the Republic of Texas. He ordered Zachary Taylor to organize an army to advance into the republic to establish a presence and indicate to Mexico the intention of the United States to hold its new territory. Heading for Corpus Christi Bay, Taylor established a beach front camp of 4,000 strong. Among the throng was Sarah's first husband, an orderly sergeant, probably by the name of Bourjett, in the Seventh Regiment of Infantry.

Following her mate and looking for excitement at the same time, Sarah gained notoriety the minute she set her huge foot on the sand. A giantess, she was a 200-pound, red-headed Amazon, who at six-foot-two towered over most of the soldiers. One soldier couldn't believe his eyes. When first casting his eyes upward at Sarah's attractive face, he thought of *The Great Western*, the first steamship in 1838 to cross the Atlantic, a 235-foot monster of the sea with twin paddle wheels and gigantic smoke stacks. "Lordee!" exclaimed the soldier as Sarah moved out of earshot. "Look at the size of her! Why she's purt' near as big as *The Great Western*!" The nickname stuck, which was good because none of her other surnames did. Old army and census records show it changed from Bourjett to Bourdette to Bouget to Davis to Borginnis and finally to Bowman.

Life was miserable on the beaches of Corpus Christi. Frigid winds, cutting sleet, and wet, unsanitary accommodations made for a winter the men would never forget. Coupled with no fresh drinking water and the lack of female company, morale was at its lowest. When Sarah came, she didn't care about the weather. She was following orders of the great commander Zachary Taylor, her hero. For the homesick, she provided comfort and to an otherwise intolerable situation, her own brand of sanity. Assigned "mess" duty for the young officers of the regiment, though her official title was "laundress," Sarah did everything from cooking to cleaning uniforms to providing pleasurable services that could never be listed on her military resume. She was an athlete who moved heavy iron cooking pots with ease and challenged any Mexican who took old Zack Taylor's name in vain. Yet, in his memoirs, one admirer describes The Great Western as "...modest and womanly not withstanding her great size and attire." He goes on to describe her flamboyant dress as reminiscent of Medieval times. "She has on a crimson velvet waist, a pretty riding skirt and her head is surmounted by a gold laced cap of the Second Artillery. She is carrying pistols and a rifle."

When General Taylor began to move his army of occupation toward the Rio Grande to a new camp near Matamoros, she was one of four women who were allowed to go. Plans were to transport the women and sick to Port Isabel while the army moved south on foot. For some unknown reason her husband went by sea. Sarah, on the other hand, chose to travel overland with her "boys." They needed her, she convinced the commanding officer. Somebody had to take care of them. In preparation for the difficult trip, Sarah purchased a mule-driven cart and in it packed her luggage, cooking utensils, and supplies. Then with whip in hand, she began the journey using skills a seasoned teamster might have envied. "During the whole journey she kept up the 'mess' a relief from the burdens of which, is the greatest boon to an officer on the march."

When the army reached the Colorado River on March 20, 1846, Mexican and American troops had a standoff. The Mexicans commanded that the U.S. dare not come any further. Sarah, infuriated by the gall of the enemy, stood on the sidelines. Then with an air of majesty, The Great Western walked out to the bank and shouted that if the General would give her a good pair of tongs, she would wade the river and whip every scoundrel that dared show himself. It was a speech that marked her a leader among men. Spurred by Sarah's bravado, the Americans charged through the shallow water only to see the backs of the enemy as they hightailed it through the brush. She could stand firm before the devil himself, and the men knew it.

Taylor continued to lead his column down Taylor's Trail, a 174-mile march from the Nueces River to the Rio Grande. Once they reached Matamoros, he built Fort Texas, which would be the setting for the first real battle between the United States and Mexico. With word that the Mexicans were threatening his supply base at Point Isabel, Taylor moved most of his men to that vital location. He commanded Major Jacob Brown to guard the fort with the help of five hundred men. The women and the sick were to stay put within the safety of the nine-foot-high walls and fifteen-foot parapets. They were not to take the offensive, as ammunition reserve was to be protected at all costs.

However, the Mexican army laid siege to the fort on May 3, 1846. All women were told to move to the "bomb-proofs" where their job was to sew sandbags. Sarah, however, wanted to stay where the action was. She chose to cook for artillery men. In the center of the fort, she prepared meals on time and carried coffee to soldiers stationed along the walls. At noon, she served bean soup. According to a period newspaper report in the *Spirit of the Times*, "This bean soup is declared by the Mexicans to be the foundation of that invincible spirit which they have seen so strikingly displayed by the Yankee soldiers. This she distributed again, without money and without price." The Mexicans then doubled their efforts. While shells exploded as they hit the fort on all sides, Sarah worked at the center of the fort, preparing meals, seeing to the wounded, and giving support to battle-weary soldiers. She even visited the artillery men who could not leave their stations and gave them nourishment and consolation. It was a nerve-jolting day with over 1,500 shells exploding in every direction.

The bombardment went on for seven days and nights. When General Arista asked for surrender, the Americans, angry over the loss of their leader, Major Brown, refused. When Arista sent in 5,000 men, Sarah asked for a musket. She would fight, she told the men, and dared any Mexican to come within her range. The siege continued with Sarah, who served meal after meal, continuing with her efforts to keep up morale. Deadly fire didn't seem to deter her from her duties. One bullet even tore through her bonnet and into her bread tray. At one point Sarah went on to distinguish herself by taking the place of a soldier killed while firing a cannon. While she manned the dead man's station, one Mexican struck her on the cheek with his saber, leaving a permanent scar she would wear with pride. Outraged, Sarah fired at point blank range, and her assailant was no more.

General Taylor, hearing the cannon fire from twenty-seven miles away, came to the rescue. By that evening, the American flag flew victoriously over the battle site. The sturdy fort, renamed after its fallen Major Brown, had withstood the blows of almost 3,000 shells. (Commander Brown would also become the namesake for Brownsville.) As for The Great Western, she earned the title "Heroine of Fort Brown." She was even asked to stand when army officials toasted her at an official party given for a Louisiana delegation in Matamoros.

Sarah loved money almost as much as the limelight. A businesswoman who couldn't write her name, Sarah knew how to make money. She understood the basic concept of supply and demand. When the army moved to Monterrey in 1846, Sarah opened up the American House, "a boarding house" that served wine, women, and song. It wasn't permanent, and soon Sarah was on the road again. When the column moved to Saltillo two months later, she never looked back but opened a second American House, the setting for brave Sarah to show her patriotism once again. One year later, 20,000 Mexicans, under the illustrious Santa Anna, attacked Taylor's 4,759 men in what was to become known as the Battle of Buena Vista. The Americans again held fast, due partly to Sarah's resolve. When some of Taylor's men panicked and ran to her, she chastised them for being so cowardly. George Washington Trahern, a Texan who was in the battle, recalled her lashing out at one trembling deserter. "You damned son of a bitch," she bellowed, "there ain't Mexicans enough in Mexico to whip old Taylor... You just spread that report and I'll beat you to death." The disgraced man returned to the column and fought bravely. With her restaurant as a makeshift hospital, Sarah, dubbed "Doctor Mary," acted as nurse for Dr. Charles M. Hitchcock and even ran onto the bloody battlefield to rescue and carry wounded back to the safety of the American House. In yet another heroic move, Sarah saved the lives of a number of soldiers who were crossing in a flatboat—it sank while she and her "adopted" children were on it.

People who knew The Great Western tended to overlook the fact that she was a prostitute. A woman to be reckoned with, she was strong yet benevolent, demanding yet supportive. When she discovered that the captain who had recruited her, George Lincoln of the Eighth Regiment, had been killed in battle, she was grief-stricken. Determined to give her friend a proper burial, she searched the battlefield until she found his body. Then she brought it to Saltillo and made funeral arrangements. When his horse went up for auction, she bought it for $250 and gave it to Lincoln's mother.

As for the sick, the hungry, or the lost, Sarah was a regular Florence Nightingale. Probably born in Tennessee, she never had any children of her own, but many an orphan called her "Mother." When the five Skinner children lost their parents, she took them into her home. Sarah also became the guardian of Olive Oatman, a child held by Indians for five years. The girl's parents and six siblings were heading west on the Santa Fe Trail when they fell victim to an Indian attack. Olive's mother and father and four of the children were killed. Olive's brother Lorenzo was left for dead while she and her sister Mary Ann, 7, were carried off and sold to Mohaves. Mary Ann died of starvation, but Olive survived to tell the tale. American soldiers succeeded in bartering for Olive and brought her to Yuma where The Great Western gladly took in the teenager. Later when traveling through central Arizona where the killings took place, Sarah took the time to locate the spot of the massacre and bury the bones of the Oatman family. Unfortunately, The Great Western wasn't as loving when it came to her Negro and Mexican servants, which were slapped and knocked down when they didn't follow instructions.

Still the Saltillo American House became the unofficial headquarters for officer and calveryman alike. It was a place where every need was met for a mere $2.50. Sarah towered over all within her domain. She orchestrated operations with one thing in mind—to provide her boys with the best of sensual pleasures. In his memoirs, Trahern remembered, "You can imagine how tall she was. She could stand flatfooted and drop these little sugar plums [her nipples] right into my mouth." Whether her husbands through the years objected to her "giving of herself" to other men is anybody's guess. During her stay in Saltillo, it wasn't long before Sally had invited a man named Davis into her private quarters on a regular basis. She later took his last name, giving some rise to the possibility that they may have married.

In the meantime, the Treaty of Guadalupe Hidalgo was signed, ending the war, and U.S. troops stationed in Mexico were once again on the move. Most were being sent to California to take possession of the new territory. It was during this move that Sarah met the man of her dreams, or so she thought. He was just her size. Called "Hercules," the man fell for Sarah, too. Sally sent Davis packing, and love was in bloom again. The newness quickly wore off, and sadly, The Great Western found that size wasn't everything. Soon the romance she thought would last forever burned itself out.

After the war, she separated from the army only to meet back up with them as she was drifting her way west. The Saltillo column ran into The Great Western as she led her small wagon train westward. Dressed in a purple velvet riding dress and sitting on a white horse, she looked majestic. When she asked Major Bucker if she could accompany the column, he reminded her that single women weren't allowed to join armed forces even for travel. By this time, Sarah had dumped her first, second, and third husbands and was currently free. He said that if she married one of the dragoons, she would be allowed to join them as a laundress. That was a solution. Giving a military salute, she rode toward the line and cried out to the men: "Who wants a wife with fifteen thousand dollars and the biggest leg in Mexico? Come, my beauties, don't all speak at once—who is the lucky man?" After a pregnant pause, one man weakly spoke up. He would marry her if a "... clergyman was present to tie the knot." Sarah laughed. "Bring your blankets to my tent tonight," she said, "and I will learn you to tie a knot that will satisfy you, I reckon!" She married the man, who never had a chance to spend any of Sarah's money. He soon followed in the footsteps of his predecessors.

When gold was discovered in California in 1848, Sarah knew that many gold-seekers would choose the southern route through El Paso on their way to the promised land. Now a civilian, she headed for the tent city that had been hastily erected to accommodate the throng of forty-niners. She knew money had wings there, and she planned to catch herself some. In April 1849, a boundary survey team for the army ran into her again as she paddled a dugout canoe toward El Paso. She threw her massive arms around each soldier, who was easily lifted off his feet. She joined them as they headed in her direction, to El Paso, where she would become the first prostitute and madam-of-record in El Paso. When she arrived, she joined forces with Benjamin Franklin Coons, and together they erected the first true structure, the Central Hotel, a restaurant-hotel-brothel in Pass City. Soon the sparse adobe huts and small stores were replaced by more permanent ones, and within months, El Paso became a popular haven for scalp hunters, trappers, soldiers, missionaries, conquistadors, wranglers, settlers, and gold miners.

When Coons left for California, Sarah kept "house" until she, too, moved in 1850 to New Mexico where the 1850 census reports that she, "Sarah Bourjette," was living with one Juan Duran and the five Skinner children. Sometime after the census, she married still another man. Though there is no official marriage record, she took a new last name and spent the next sixteen years living as the wife of Sergeant Albert Bowman. They moved to Arizona, where the restless madam opened and closed brothels in a variety of settlements that sprang up overnight. Bowman, a German-born lad a decade younger than his wife, must have also had wanderlust. Together they set up a number of businesses in New Mexico and Arizona. Yuma must have felt more like home, as they stayed there the longest. Located near a busy ferry crossing, the Bowmans operated a "boarding house," restaurant, and saloon. Sarah also began keeping "mess" for officers stationed there. Later Bowman and Sarah moved to Gila City, a desert stop for '49ers; but being a camp follower at heart, Sarah heard the sounds of Fort Buchanan at Sonoita Creek. By 1860 she had said "adios" to Albert, leaving him in a cloud of Arizona dust.

Sarah once said that "... there was just one thin sheet of sandpaper between Yuma and Hell." In spite of the fact that she was happy with her lot, the years and the harsh land finally took its toll on her appearance. Her indomitable spirit, however, prevailed until her life was shortened prematurely by an insect bite at the age of 53. How ironic that a huge tarantula spider, small in comparison to The Great Western, should claim her on Dec. 23, 1866. She was buried with full military honors, a dedicated patriot who had been awarded a full army pension for her feats of bravery. According to 1860 records, Sarah had accumulated $2,000 worth of real estate, a formidable sum considering her era and occupation. The body of The Great Western was later moved from the deteriorating Fort Yuma federal cemetery to Presidio, California, where her tombstone sits proudly surrounded by those of "her boys." Researcher Brian Sandwich, author of *The Great Western*, reports that when Sarah's remains were being moved, a very large Catholic medal, one appropriate for a person of grand stature, was found in her grave, testimony once again to her immense size.

A complex personality, Sarah Bourjett Davis Bowman was a restless spirit whose home was wherever she happened to pitch her tent. Her roots never had a chance to take hold in one given spot, yet her "stand tall" memory has been preserved in the writings of "her boys" who loved her. Her sobriquet, "The Great Western," is fitting, for in her own way, she helped to perpetuate the great movement westward to new horizons.

Note: Little has been written about The Great Western. Most of the information here comes from author Brian Sandwich, who in 1991 published the biography, *The Great Western: Legendary Lady of the Southwest,* for the University of Texas at El Paso.

LOTTIE DENO

Lady Luck Lottie

possibly 1844-1934

It was an ugly town with an uglier name—"The Flat." Everybody from mean-tempered buffalo hunters to cold-blooded gunslingers used it as their watering hole. Blasé saloon girls scratched out a living there, and each night quick-handed gamblers pocketed silver and gold. It was a den of iniquity where temptation always won over temperance. Sitting in the shadows of Fort Griffin, The Flat, as it was nicknamed, was the self-proclaimed "wickedest town on earth." In fact, its residents boasted of having "a man for breakfast every morning." A government post, Indian reservation, supply base for cattlemen heading up the Western Trail, and headquarters for buffalo hunting outfits, the town called to everyone who ventured into its lurid realm, like the siren of Shackelford County waiting for her prey.

Among some of the well-known names strolling the notorious streets of The Flat were Wyatt Earp, John H. "Doc" Holliday, "Bat" Masterson, John Wesley Hardin, and John Selman. Earp is thought to have gone there to elicit Doc Holliday's help in hunting down gunslinger Dade Rudabaugh. Hardin boasted of 40 notches on his gun before John Selman shot him in El Paso. Another infamous visitor to The Flat was "Big Nose" Kate Elder, Holliday's woman, who later swung from a tree for cattle rustling in Montana.

And yet, among all the flotsam of The Flat, the most popular character was the mysterious Concho Country Poker Queen, Lottie Deno. A Kentucky belle with a quiet sense of southern decorum, Lottie was a study in contrast to most who sat at her green-felted table. She was a curious sight to behold as she shuffled the pasteboards with detachment for shady characters quick on the draw. Some said she was Lady Luck personified, majestic yet merciless. Few could ruffle her richly attired exterior.

For gamblers like Lottie, The Flat meant money. A parasite settlement where greenbacks flowed freely, The Flat sprouted like a weed below on the flat, or wide "second bottom" of Clear Fork, a tributary of the Brazos River. A handful of stone buildings with mud roofs clung precariously to each other as they braced for an element of civilization that walked on the wild side. On a high hill overlooking a bend in Clear Fork, Fort Griffin was an anchor, a new line of defense established during Reconstruction. Its duty was to protect settlers from the Indians. In general, Fort Griffin was the most miserable fort assignment for any soldier, no matter what his rank. In 1874 the commanding officer wrote that the post was unfit for human habitation. With abhorrent living conditions and dreadful food, troops condemned to life there were ready to fight anybody—redskins, renegades, and even the bugler blowing reveille.

These soldiers served in every decisive campaign against the tribes of the Western Plains. This was because Fort Griffin was a key rendezvous and supply depot for Ronald Mackenzie's Red River Campaign against the Comanche and Kiowa Indians. Not only did the dusty soil soak up the blood of an Indian nation, but this fort also marked the spot where a wild, senseless slaughter wiped out the great southern herd of American bison.

For the homesick soldier, The Flat provided the only means of entertainment. Officers and underlings mixed freely, and rank was put aside as they drank, gambled, laughed, and argued together. Countless others added color

Lottie Deno   (Photo courtesy of Fort Concho National Historic Landmark, San Angelo, Texas.)

to the lurid tone. Cowpokes and mule skinners flocked to Fort Griffin by droves. And, with the massacre of the bison, buffalo hides became big business. During 1877 about 200,000 hides were shipped through The Flat, called "Hide City" by the hunters. This was also a time when astute businessmen realized they were exterminating their source of income. Smart money was shifted to cattle. In one month alone, more than 50,000 beeves were driven along the Western Trail headed to Dodge City stockyards. With each sunset, crowds buzzed into the Wilson and Matthew Saloon and Shaunessey's popular Bee Hive. Everyone, eager to wash away the trail dust, spent his hard-earned wage as if The Flat would never see another dawn. Lawlessness, however, became so flagrant in The Flat that a band of vigilantes formed. Calling themselves the Old Law Mob, they kept ropes handy for the undesirable element who refused to leave town. Corpses of those who chose not to heed the warnings were regularly found sprawled in the street with a note attached. It simply read, "O.L.M."

During those wild days in Fort Griffin, a mysterious woman appeared one day out of a clouded past. She arrived by the Jacksboro stage in the spring of 1877 sitting up on the box beside driver Dick Wheeler. The waiting crowd stared agog at the striking lady, whose expensive attire hinted of big city society. Her demeanor was one of sophistication and class.

Old-timers remember that when she checked into the hotel, she wrote only her name, "Lottie Deno," in the register. Miss Deno listed no address. Apparently, she decided not to use her alias, "Mystic Maude." That name belonged to a time now passed, a period in Santa Angela (now San Angelo) where she had made herself known as a formidable lady gambler. Who she was really, nobody knew. Gossip and speculation circulated for decades, fueled by the enigmatic woman herself, who gave few facts about her background. As a result, fact and fiction formed a legendary *femme fatale* of the gaming tables who continues to mystify even to this day.

Those who knew Lottie said she had black, dancing eyes. Portly, yet attractive, she possessed classic features that were framed by heavy, dark luxuriant hair. Though not a raving beauty, she had a way with men, who fell smitten by her charms. Lawman John Jacobs, who actually knew Lottie, described her as "a wonderful woman" with attractive features, and most who knew Lottie tended to agree. He says she was not a prostitute. On the other hand, Henry Herron, a deputy sheriff in Fort Griffin and also Lottie's contemporary, seemed a bit sour in his assessment of her. He says Lottie, a "wicked" wanderer who engaged her clientele in much more than a friendly game of cards, was "good looking, but I would hardly call her pretty." The evaluations of the two lawmen make for curious contradiction and probably explain why historians are divided on the issue of whether Lottie flew with soiled doves.

Whatever her job description, Lottie had old family breeding. Some of her acquaintances remembered a faint French accent, lending to the popular story that the poker queen was really the daughter of a rich Louisiana plantation owner. John Jacobs, however, in an interview with his friend J. Marvin Hunter, says much about Lottie's past. The gambler's confidant, Jacobs called her a "lone wolf operator" who had little to do with the common prostitutes who worked the saloons. She told Jacobs that her real name was not Lottie Deno. Born in Warsaw, Kentucky, she was the daughter of a prominent couple. Her father was an outstanding turfman of the Blue Grass State who won sweepstakes purses with his many blooded race horses. His chief jockey was wildly extravagant, the son of a Georgia gambler who was always in trouble. Lottie went against her parents' wishes and married the young man. To her dismay, her parents cut ties.

For the years following, she and her husband, who also turned to gambling, traveled around the country. He taught Lottie the tricks of the trade, and she became expert. *(In some versions of the Lottie Deno story, her father taught her how to play. She sharpened her skills in Europe while casino hopping with her family. There she watched the best in the world work the cards to their advantage. Then the Civil War claimed her father and the family fortune. To care for her stroke-plagued mother and send her little sister to a high-class boarding school, Lottie headed to the Detroit casinos. Later she made her way down to the action in Santa*

Angela and settled for a while there, where she lived a life of a recluse by day and a professional gambler by night.)

Jacobs tells Hunter that months before Lottie stepped off the stagecoach into the dust of The Flat, her husband had killed a man during a card game. On the run, he took all of Lottie's cash and headed for Mexico, leaving Lottie destitute. Lottie went on to tearfully tell the lawman that her husband had located her and wanted to join her in San Angelo. She hastily left there to start a new life and wound up in The Flat.

Her husband didn't find her in Fort Griffin, and before long everyone had lost money to Lottie. In those smoke-filled Texas saloons, she kept her wits always about her even in the nastiest of presence. Amid the debauchery, Lottie played an honest game and stayed away from liquor and high stake pots where guns lay ready on the table. She kept acquaintances at arm's length during the day by drawing shut her shades and locking her doors. Only on occasion did she allow certain gambling gentlemen into her shanty on Concho Street for a secluded game of faro or poker. And, at times, a matronly woman from the fort would also visit Lottie at her home.

Almost every night Lottie, dressed in a lavish gown, flipped the pasteboards at the Bee Hive. Over the saloon door, a sign read:

Within this Hive, we are alive;
Good whisky makes us funny.
Get your horse tied, come inside,
And taste the flavor of our honey.

The Bee Hive was owned by John Shaunessey, a man who would later bring grief to Lottie.

It was at the Wilson and Matthew Saloon, however, where the legend of Lottie Deno truly emerged. One October night, Lottie was working a $50-limit game in the corner when nasty words flew between Monte Bill, an Arizona gambler, and Smoky Joe, a Texas high roller. In a cutthroat game, Monte Bill suggested they raise the limit, and Smoky, down to his last dollar, decided to go for all or broke. The stakes were over $500 when the Arizona shark turned three aces and a pair of queens, a full house.

Curses flew, Smoky dropped his hand to the handle of his six-shooter and yelled, "Bunkoed by a sneaking coyote from the Badlands, who rings in a cold deck and marked cards when he plays with a gentleman! Take the pot, John," he called to the Negro porter. The Arizonian yelled back, "No, you can't play that game of bluff on me!" Shots blazed and patrons scrambled madly from the room—all except Lottie. She pushed back from the table and went to the corner of the room out of the line of fire. When the smoke cleared and the bloodied men lay ready for their trip to Boot Hill, Lottie stood composed, cards still in hand. She had witnessed the melee with thoughtful detachment.

When the sheriff arrived, he asked her, "Why didn't you vamoose when they pulled their barkers, Lottie?" "Oh, it was too late, sheriff, and I was safe out of range in the corner," the gambler assured him. "Well, you have your nerve on, all right, old girl. I don't believe I would have cared to take my chances in that scrimmage," said the lawman. "Perhaps not, sheriff," Lottie said, "but you are not a desperate woman."

Lottie probably figured the odds of getting shot a second time were slim. A few years before, she took a stray bullet in the eye which was permanently blinded as a result. The Old West expression, "Out like Lottie's eye" came from the incident. One source says that sometime later, after questioning the saloon's patrons, the sheriff thought to look for the money that had been on the table. Had Lottie's purse bulged conspicuously? He had waited too late to question her, and the money was never found.

But, according to Sheriff Jacobs, Lottie was honest and would help with the apprehension of those up to no good. When she found herself privy to outlaw talk, she always passed the information on to him. Though she stayed out of trouble most of the time, she was once fined $100 for "maintaining a disorderly house." Herron uses this as ammunition for his criticism that the gambler seconded as a prostitute. Jacobs doesn't whitewash her altogether, however. He remembered one time when Lottie lost her cool head and reached for her gun. The incident revolved around the infamous Doc Holliday, her good friend. Big Nose Kate, a notorious character known for a lewd lifestyle, accused Lottie of trying to steal her man, Doc. "Why, you low-down slinking slut!" screamed Lottie, "If I should step in soft cow manure, I would not even clean my foot on that bastard! I'll show you a thing or two!" Doc stopped a shoot-out by standing between the two.

Love proved the end of Lottie's career in The Flat. Lottie was considered the sweetheart of an ill-tempered bartender, Shaunessey, and no man dared interfere. Then the daring Johnny Golden arrived. Reports vary as to Johnny Golden's background, but general contention is that Lottie and he knew each other as gamblers who met in the Midwest. Of wealthy Bostonian stock, Johnny also had style, but his breeding still didn't compare to Lottie's. Johnny, though, had charisma coupled with handsome features, and that made him a heart-stealer. Lottie must have fallen for his charms. They separated for some reason only to meet once again at Fort Griffin. *(Jacobs says Johnny was a shady character who he believed ". . . held some kind of club over her." He says she told him Johnny knew her husband's troubles, and she had to keep him pacified.)* Most, however, believe their relationship was full of passion and fury. Some speculate that Golden was a low life who associated with outlaws. Whatever the truth, Lottie went from the arms of Shaunessey and into Johnny's.

Their time together was short-lived, as death came calling for Johnny Golden. One story centers on the jealous John Shaunessey, who supposedly loved Lottie. Outraged, Shaunessey vowed to get his competition. One night, deputy sheriff Jim Draper and town marshal Bill Gilson came after Johnny, who was spending the evening at Shaunessey's Saloon. When they stood before witnesses and falsely accused him of horse stealing, he denied any wrongdoing. "I've never even owned a horse," he explained. They arrested him anyway, told him they were taking him to the military guardhouse, and led him outside to the dark street. Twenty yards from the saloon, they shot him. Johnny's body was found behind Hank Smith's wagon yard. The lawmen first said a mob killed him. Then they said he was trying to break away, and they shot him. Friends of the dead man found that a bullet had gone through the body and then down into the ground. Golden, they surmised, had been lying on his back when he was shot. Talk was Shaunessey had paid the men $250 to eliminate his competition. The day after the shooting, the lawmen faced a justice of the peace hearing only to be exonerated on flimsy evidence. Golden's father later came to Texas to find out what really happened to his son. When he arrived in Fort Worth, the elder Golden not only received a chilly reception, but his life was threatened. Shaken, he returned home without the facts.

When Lottie heard the news, she broke into hysterical weeping—the only public display of emotion The Flat had ever seen from her. She blamed herself for Golden's death. When funeral arrangements were being made, Lottie came to Jacobs with $65, enough to pay for a new suit, a coffin, and other funeral expenses. She couldn't bring herself to attend the services, however, but she probably couldn't help but look out her window as the procession with eight mourners passed in front of her house. Among those in attendance was Bill Gilson, one of Golden's shooters. From that day on, she went into seclusion with all supplies brought to her by delivery.

One month later, Lottie asked Jacobs if he would sell her a small leather-bound trunk with brass trimmings and clasp that he had purchased in Kentucky. He sold it to her and watched as she had the stage driver load this sole piece of luggage on the Fort Concho-bound coach. Some believed she carried in it winnings of around $20,000. She told Jacobs she was going to meet up with her husband. Once the stagecoach pulled away, everyone wanted to see what Lottie had left behind, but no one dared enter the little house. With her rent paid up for one month, it was best to wait for the authorities.

When the new sheriff, Bill Cruger, returned from Albany, he opened the door to Lottie Deno's secret world. The room was decorated with the finest of furniture, fabric, and fancy bed linens. On the bed was pinned a note that read, "Sell this outfit and give the money to someone in need of assistance." Lottie Deno vanished that day. With her she took a broken heart, many said, for she really did love her Johnny. Shaunessey also left Fort Griffin some months later. He sold his place and then took off for Palo Pinto, where he opened another saloon. Whether his path crossed with Lottie's is anybody's guess.

It wasn't until 1881, when the army closed the fort, that a deadly calm took over the streets of The Flat. With the soldiers and buffalo gone, there was no longer any need to come there. Even the Comanches were killed off at Palo Duro Canyon, and the big cattle drives were over. Fort Griffin and its offspring of iniquity sank without a whimper into the bowels of the earth.

As for Lottie, Hunter claims he knew Lottie as Charlotta Thurmond in Deming, New Mexico, around 1900 when she lived next-door to him. She was married to Frank Thurmond, a wealthy man from Georgia. Whether Frank was the Georgia jockey and gambler is unknown, but Deming old-timers advised Hunter to never engage in a friendly game of cards with the Thurmonds. Hunter said that Mrs. Thurmond was a sweet individual who showed him every kindness, that she lived a long life dedicating herself to charity. When she died, stories of her past life as the Poker Queen of the West emerged, though no one could prove her true identity. For J. Marvin Hunter, however, the mystery of Lottie Deno was solved, for at the auction sale of the effects of Mrs. Charlotta Thurmond, deceased, Deming, New Mexico, a small leather-bound trunk with brass trimmings and clasp went on the block. At his death, J. Marvin Hunter owned a little piece of Fort Griffin history.

"MA" (Miriam Amanda) FERGUSON

"Two Governors for the Price of One"

1875-1961

The Texas political tide was turning against Governor Jim Ferguson during his second term of office. It all started with the University of Texas. Angry with school regents over their refusal to remove certain faculty members he found objectionable, he decided to teach *them* a lesson. When the school's appropriation bill crossed his desk, he vetoed their funding. Longhorns everywhere, particularly those in high places, were outraged. His enemies took the incident and ran with it, and by 1917, the state legislature was accusing him of embezzlement, misapplication of public funds, and failing to properly enforce banking laws of the state. He looked ahead to the impeachment proceedings with dread. Surely his public would see that he was a victim of a kangaroo court. Everything he had worked for was washing away down a river of betrayal, and he felt helpless to stop it.

He thought of Miriam, his wife, with her soft features, luminous eyes, and kind manner. He knew she would stand behind him through this fiasco. Suddenly, he hit upon a stroke of political genius. He would run Miriam in his place. A belle of Belton society, she would represent stability to the hard-working blue collar populace. She was a true southerner and mother figure all rolled into one. And, besides, a vote for her would be a vote for him. She would take the governor's chair, and he would stand in the shadows behind her, orchestrating. Everything, he thought, was going to be all right after all. Sitting on the side of a bed in a Taylor, Texas, hotel room, "Farmer Jim" made the announcement. Miriam Ferguson will be the next governor of the great state of Texas.

Only in the Lone Star State, some said, could a man be impeached but still remain a key figure in the governor's office. Jim knew that if anybody could do it, he could. But he was plagued by strong opposition. The Ku Klux Klan hated him. The women suffragists disdainfully saw him as he truthfully was—"a good old boy." As for the media, it was leery of both Fergusons. One Texas newspaper editor stated that apparently "Texas is not too old to have a governess," while the *Albany News* made fun of Miriam. It pictured the Ferguson wash as it blew in the wind behind the Capitol, while Miriam was forced to put down her knitting to see to matters of state.

Yet, Jim believed Miriam could charm the working class. For the farmers, the mechanics, and the factory workers, she represented the backbone of simple, Christian life. His wife's easy personality coupled with his flamboyant political maneuvers, backwoods intuition, and public savvy made them sure winners. "Farmer Jim" capitalized on the folksy image and played it to the hilt for Texas voters. And, when reporter Frank Gibler of the *Houston Post* quickly combined Miriam Amanda's first and middle initials to nickname her "Ma," Jim seized on the campaign theme. If they couldn't have "Pa," voters could certainly get "Ma."

Feminists of her day were suspicious. When some of Ma's supporters encouraged her to be more than a figurehead for Jim, she pledged allegiance to her husband. Crowds who gathered at the town squares for campaign speeches heard Jim, rather than Miriam. "You'll get two governors for the price of one . . . I'll tell her what to sign and what not to sign," he always said. At that, Miriam always added mechanically, "A vote for me is a vote for my husband." When Ma saw that an audience was composed of men who wanted no part of an

"Governors Jim and Ma Ferguson with the common people." *(Photo courtesy of the Austin History Center, Austin Public Library.)*

intelligent, liberated woman, she played the part of the subservient wife. She explained to them that she had originally not been in favor of women voting, but that she used this new right to cast her support for her husband in his unsuccessful bid for the United States Senate in 1922. On the other hand, Miriam used the woman's vote to her advantage. With women being granted the right to mark a ballot in 1920, the Miriam Ferguson candidacy appealed to those active in the suffrage movement.

The campaign took on a theatrical quality, filled with one gimmick after another. Jim tirelessly organized photo shoots depicting his wife in her sunbonnet feeding her prize Leghorns or in her kitchen canning peaches. The 1924 campaign featured back-home slogans like "Me for Ma" bumper stickers and the blatant "Two Governors for the Price of One." Anti-Klan voters, who wanted secrecy stripped from the racist organization, were asked to choose between "The sunbonnet or the hood." Poems such as this one circulated in the country stores, barbershops, and at church socials:

> *Hoods off!*
> *Along the street there comes*
> *Patriotic daughters and loyal sons,*
> *A crowd of bonnets beneath the sky,*
> > *Hoods off!*
> *Miriam Ferguson is passing by.*
>
> *Get out your old-time bonnet*
> *And put Miriam Ferguson on it,*
> > *And hitch your wagon to a star.*
> *So on election day*
> *We each of us can say*
> > *Hurrah! Governor Miriam, Hurrah!*

"Put on Your Old Gray Bonnet" became Miriam's campaign song, and Houston women asked for patterns of the "Ma Ferguson" sunbonnet.

The strategy worked and gave the Fergusons two more administrations in Austin. As for "Ma," she became the first woman governor of Texas and the second in America. And though everybody knew Miriam didn't win the governorship on her own merit, she had some impact on state government. She and Pa brought country color into the state house. On her Inauguration Day, January 20, 1925, the band blared out her campaign song, "Put On Your Old Gray Bonnet," and her constituents arrived for her speech in their Fords and horse-drawn wagons to applaud "Ma." Dressed in a black satin suit trimmed with chinchilla fur, the forty-nine-year-old governor wore a draped boa of spidery white feathers. Crowning her finery was a large black hat sprouting bird feathers. No fashion editor ever referred to "Ma" as chic, but she did have her own style.

According to writer Maisie Paulissen, Judge Few Brewster, a one-time neighbor of Miriam, remembers her as a little rough around the edges. "Those were the days when a vegetable man used to roll his cart down the street and sell his produce to the housewives," explains the judge. He goes on to say that Miriam would cup her hands to her mouth and yell, "You got any muskmelons?" and the vendor would yell back, "We ain't got muskmelons, we got wattymelons," and she would answer, "Don't need wattymelons."

Actually, Miriam Amanda Wallace grew up in a fine house in Belton with an extremely indulgent father who wouldn't have let his daughter go near a chicken yard. She even attended college, the Baylor Female College in Belton, and was a rarity for the times—an educated woman. Miriam Amanda was also a member of the prestigious Daughters of the Republic of Texas and the United Daughters of the Confederacy. Her father, Joseph Wallace, enlisted in the Confederate army at the outbreak of the Civil War and returned to Texas only after Lee's surrender. Joseph Wallace believed in doing his duty to the end and taught his daughter to stick to her obligations.

There were no silver spoons in Jim's family. He came from a poor family that knew the meaning of hard work. His father died when Jim was four years old. Life for them was a constant struggle for survival. As soon as he was old enough, he worked alongside his mother on the family farm. At sixteen he left home and headed for the West, taking jobs where he found them. A couple of years later, he returned to Bell County where he briefly studied law. Actually, Jim's tale was a real Horatio Alger story, for he passed the bar exam using borrowed notebooks. A brand new smooth-talking lawyer, he was destined for politics.

Miriam met Jim when her father died. Joseph Wallace left his family a tidy sum of money, stock, property, and cotton gins. When Miriam's mother needed help settling the estate, she called the young James E. Ferguson, a distant relative. Jim was fond of telling audiences how it was love at first sight when he saw Miriam at the Wallace home. Miriam, however, was not anxious to marry a poor young lawyer, and when Jim asked for her hand, she promptly turned him down. Using his gift of eloquent speech, he persisted until, finally, Miriam Amanda gave in to his pleas. They were married on December 31, 1899, the last day of the nineteenth century. The pair prospered, and fifteen years later, Jim was the most important man in the state.

"Ma" and "Pa" were a matched pair. Jim, governor in 1914 and reelected in 1916, also considered himself a champion of the farmer. When the announcement was made that Jim was going to be impeached, "the boys at the forks of the creeks" held firm their confidence in Jim. Life as governor, however, was over for him. Even when his 1916 campaign was in progress, certain "irregularities" in conduct cited by Ferguson critics began to surface, marring his political future. Ferguson was finally indicted on nine charges which grew to twenty-one articles of impeachment, all relating to the mishandling of money and public funds. By an overwhelming vote of twenty-five to three, the Court of Impeachment removed Ferguson and made him ineligible to hold any office of honor, trust, or profit under the state of Texas. Many Texans felt that he had been railroaded. They just "didn't have a dern thing against Pa, so they elected Ma."

As the state's First Lady and a fervent teetotaler, Ma never allowed alcohol in the Governor's Mansion. Nor did she permit swearing or card playing. No matter who was being entertained at the governor's table, Miriam Amanda never broke her strict rules. Six o'clock sharp marked the dinner hour. Even as governor, she changed little in the household routine except that she and Jim spent most of their evenings quietly working. The Ferguson daughters, Ouida and Dorrace, were strictly disciplined, and boyfriends had to leave promptly at ten o'clock. In her columns in the Ferguson political mouthpiece, the *Ferguson Forum*, Ma conveyed views that went from the progressive, with women having the right to enter the work force, to the old-fashioned, where women stayed at home to be wives and mothers. And under no condition should a woman smoke "cigareetes."

During Ma's first term, two desks sat side-by-side in her office. One belonged to Jim, her "advisor and confidant," as she called him. The number one priority on Ma's agenda was passing the Amnesty Bill of 1925 which would restore full political rights to Jim. It was later ruled unconstitutional, and Jim had to be content to run the state through Miriam. The voters really did get "two governors for the price of one."

Controversy plagued Ma's administrations as well. She angered the Klan by forcing them to remove their masks in public. They countered by attacking Miriam. She was only fit, they said, for the business of being a wife and mother or for feeding her chickens. Did she really have the power of the governorship, or did she allow Jim to make all the decisions? Opinions differed among staff members. Some said Ma really was in control, yet others contended Jim held the real power. The truth was that Miriam allowed her husband to write her speeches, attend her meetings, and take charge of visiting dignitaries. She supported Jim in whatever decisions he made. The highlight of her first day in office was not a meeting with her new staff or the deliberation of an important issue. Rather, it was the social she hosted for the press who stopped by the mansion for hot biscuits and peach preserves. She was, in fact, a southern belle first and foremost. Ann F. Crawford and Crystal S. Ragsdale in their *Women in Texas* say: "She applauded the comfort of modern female garments and advocated that women cut their hair and wear it in any style that suited them but warned them that when they smoked, it did not look right. She spoke out strongly in favor of jazz and of young people dancing, but also extolled the virtues of rural country living, a diet of turnip greens and cornbread, the delights of gardening, and 'our old Black Mammies.'"

Jailbirds loved the governors. Together the Fergusons pardoned one hundred prisoners per month. "They're on the take," said critics. Governor Miriam wrote out pardons faster than she wrote party invitations. The family enjoyed outings to the Huntsville State Prison. Prisoners would sit with Ma and Pa under tall shade trees and spin their sad tales. Dorrace Ferguson Watt, one of the Ferguson daughters, tells the story to Maisie Paulissen for her Ma Ferguson chapter in *Legendary Ladies of Texas*: "The first thing my mother would ask was, 'Well, what did you do?' Dad suggested that it would be better if she asked what they were charged with. And my mother answered, 'If they hadn't done something they wouldn't be here.'" Many of the prisoners, however, were jailed because they had committed liquor law violations. Since Jim had never been a prohibitionist, he favored them. Miriam thought the opposite, resulting in a number of family arguments.

Although the Fergusons seemed genuinely concerned over the plight of prisoners, the bribery rumors began to fly around Miriam. With the right payoff, some said, Ma would issue any pardon. Some friends saw the governor as merely tenderhearted, but her enemies thought the worse—she was well supplementing the meager governor's salary. Nola Wood, who once worked for Miriam, told Ms. Paulissen that she remembers cash flowing freely into the Ferguson coffers for signed pardons: "This fellow come in with a great roll of newspapers under his hat . . . And then, he'd come in with these men and in a big newspaper like this with the money all spread out, spread out on a big table like that—the money—and they'd pick it out whatever they wanted . . . a roll of bills . . . fives and tens."

Unaffected by her critics, she kept signing those pardons. Also, Ma caught heat when she appointed Jim head of the Highway Department. At the end of her first term, an investigation into the Highway Department resulted in accusations against Jim for bribing officials, taking kickbacks on contracts, and owning a company that worked for the state. Furious at attacks on her husband, Ma pardoned 33 rapists, 133 murderers, 124 robbers, and 127 liquor violators. Ma and Pa lost the next two elections in 1926 and 1928 to Dan Moody. Jim's retort was "Never say 'die,' say 'damn.'"

Undaunted, Ma ran against businessman Ross Sterling in 1930. He beat her, only to give the governor's chair back to Ma in 1932. Jim openly told the voters, "Don't worry, folks, I'll be on hand to help Mama. I'll be picking up chips and bringing in the water!" Soon twin desks appeared in the governor's office once more.

What the Fergusons found when they returned to the Governor's Mansion in 1932 was a Texas in terrible financial shape, a victim of the Great Depression. To stop the momentum of upcoming bankruptcy, Miriam Amanda closed the banks for "Texas Independence Week" on March 3, 1933. She had no authority to take the step, but it worked. When Mrs. Ferguson's executive secretary, Ghent Sanderford, asked by whose legal right, Jim handed him a proclamation he had just written for his wife. It read, "I, Governor Miriam Ferguson, by virtue of the authority assumed by me, do hereby order all the banks in the state of Texas closed indefinitely." Nearly every bank closed without questioning her order and remained shut for three days. The state avoided financial ruin, thanks to their novel yet highly illegal idea.

Governor Miriam Amanda Ferguson decided not to run for re-election in 1934, much to the surprise of her enemies and her supporters. Her rather vague reason was that the Fergusons had been in the Mansion long enough. In the Bible she presented to James V. Allred, her successor, she marked the verse: "And the most proud shall stumble and fall and none shall raise him up . . . " *Jeremiah 50:32.*

In 1940, at age 65, Ma threw her bonnet back into the ring. She should have remembered her advice to Allred because she lost to W. Lee O'Daniel. Ma's political career wasn't done for, however. She used her influence to swing a senatorial election for a future president of the United States—Lyndon B. Johnson. As for the suffrage leaders, they called her a "slave wife" and a "mere figurehead," so it's understandable that she won't go down in history as a supporter of the woman's movement. One newspaper columnist wrote an appropriate epitaph for Miriam Ferguson —"Too Much Husband." He hit dead center.

Jim died in 1944 still unable to hold public office in Texas. The controversy over whether Ma was governor in her own right or whether Jim ran the show will probably never be settled, but on her 80th birthday, 300 politicians honored her with a banquet. Miriam died of a heart attack June 25, 1961. She is buried where she should be—beside her husband. One thing is certain. The Governors Ferguson cooked up the rules to suit their own palates. As for Ma Ferguson's kitchen, well, she left it spotless. Too bad that couldn't be said for her administration.

FRENCHY McCORMICK
(Elizabeth McGraw)
The Last Girl of the Golden West
1852-1941

A funeral cortege of 22 cars drove mournfully down the icy road to Tascosa. It passed Boot Hill and then down the lonely road where the McCormicks' crumbling adobe shack still sat after sixty years, shaded by an ancient cottonwood tree. The procession turned toward the town's ghostly main street and then on to the once infamous Hogstown. The drivers finally came to a stop at the Casimiro Romero Cemetery, and against the bitter cold, doors opened, and faithful friends, determined to keep their promise, poured out. There was a biting freeze that dreary day in January 1941, as the north wind of the Texas Plains slashed through to the marrow of every bone. Slowly and reverently, as children from Cal Farley's Boys Ranch sang "Home on the Range," mourners lowered the coffin of Frenchy McCormick, who had come to rest with her beloved "Mack." That week, the Panhandle newspapers and newscasters reported the passing of "the last girl of the golden west. " At last Frenchy, once a glittering dance hall queen, would turn to dust, mixing with that of her man. Yet their love story is a legacy that lives in the hearts of those who knew them.

"No one will ever find out who I am," she vowed over one hundred years ago, and though a century's worth of historians have tried to uncover her true identity, Frenchy went to her grave without divulging a clue. From the minute she arrived in the rip-roaring cow town of Tascosa in 1880, people wondered who she really was. All they knew was that she was born in 1852 around Baton Rouge, Louisiana, and that for some unknown reason, she had run away when she was just 14.

Naturally, many versions of Frenchy's youth circulated among the town gossips who filled the lonely evenings on the prairie with local chatter. She lost her mother when she was very young, went one tale. Rather than be left at home, she took her father's steamboat and traveled with him as he traded cotton along the Mississippi. They quarreled. The pair just couldn't agree on Frenchy's future, but the young girl was adamant. Hearing the call of the theater, she wanted to perform. Her father wouldn't hear of such a disgraceful profession, but Frenchy defied him by dancing on a burlesque stage in St. Louis. Catching her in the act, he stopped her and caused a schism that could never be mended. She broke her family ties forever, turning a tearful eye from the bayous of Louisiana, and hopped a Dodge City stage. Apparently she followed her dream, and she became one of the throng who heard that Kansas was booming as a trail herd center. In still another often told story with a different twist, Frenchy was a sweet young girl, educated in a Baton Rouge convent, who fell in love with a man her father hated. Frenchy ran away with the scoundrel to St. Louis, only to find herself deserted in a strange place. Unable to face the music back home, she headed for the frontier and a new life as an entertainer.

Frenchy had heard the distant call of the Panhandle, where coins, like quicksilver, slid from one skillful hand to another across gaming tables. Saloons were cropping up faster than the spin of the roulette wheel. At first, Dodge City had been an exciting cowboy town, but she had seen enough of its dusty, barren landscape. Known for the original Boot Hill, Dodge City would not be *her* final resting place. She would not wind up like those reckless souls who lay in their

Mickey and Frenchy McCormick   (Photos courtesy of Cal Farley's Boys Ranch.)

graves with their boots on. For Frenchy, the easiest thing
about life in Kansas was leaving it. The lawless towns of the
Texas Panhandle had their Boot Hills, too, but it was the
promised land for gamblers, singers, and bartenders. She
would head for Mobeetie, where wranglers and buffalo hunters found the town accessible to the Red River and streams of
lonely soldiers from nearby Fort Elliott found solace in
Mobeetie's night life. In trunks, she packed her jewelry and
plumes, her ball gowns and ensembles, and her tiny satin
slippers, possessions that she would cherish for a lifetime. As
they were loaded on the southbound stage, she said goodbye
to a town that had grown to love her.

When she reached Mobeetie, it was obvious no one there
had ever encountered one so cultured. No doubt Frenchy's

superior education far outshone any girl in town. She wrote in a beautiful script and spoke a second language, fluent French, yet she headed straight to the saloon, where she was hired on the spot. Everybody was awestruck by her beauty.

"I want to dance with Frenchy!" yelled a cowboy one evening who saw her dancing with another man. The nickname stuck, and her popularity quickly grew. Soon she became the mystery beauty of the bayou, though a few casual acquaintances knew that Frenchy, with her sparkling blue eyes and black curly hair, was actually Irish. Early pictures show her to be quite lovely as a young Dodge City saloon girl who caught the watering eye of every cowpoke west of the Big Muddy.

It was no wonder that the mysterious beauty from southern Louisiana turned the debonair head of gambler Mickey McCormick, but Lady Luck was always on Mickey's side. A successful jack-of-all-trades who was fitted for the frontier, this Irishman made money with all he touched. He understood that a man must be versatile in order to get ahead, so when he wasn't playing the pasteboards, he hunted for pay. Hardworking and likable, he also purchased a livery stable in Tascosa, situated about 100 miles up the Canadian River from Mobeetie. For Mickey, Mobeetie meant easy pocket money. More often than not, he won big stakes at cards, especially when Frenchy sat at his side. He called her his charm, and when it came time for his return by buggy to Tascosa, Frenchy and her trunks went with him. Together they headed down the trail of a love affair that would last a lifetime.

The barren High Plains of West Texas can be ruthless. Panhandlers can't decide which is worse—the winter blizzards or the summer's searing heat. The eternal wind never ceases, whether it's piercing your skin with freezing temperatures or frying your skin to rawhide toughness with blistering gusts. But Tascosa, a cattle business boomtown, was brand new, and Mickey's livery stable was a bonanza. Always the entrepreneur, he rented out horses and carriages and carried passengers and supplies to other remote towns. To supple-

ment his growing income, he also moved gambling operations to rooms behind Main Street's Lady Gay saloon. Every
"top gun" drifter tried his quick hand when he drew from the
deck of Frenchy McCormick. And while Mickey claimed
house winnings, Frenchy also dealt for the noble and notorious alike, from Pat Garrett and Bat Masterson to Billy the Kid.
The game of the day was the popular monte, an Old West
version but not quite in the league with poker. Monte was
played with only 40 cards, and players bet against the dealer.
Those who remember Frenchy say that even when she was
old and deaf, she could not only dance a combination from
her stage days, but she could also deal a deck with lightning
speed.

In 1881, when it was just five years old, Tascosa became
the county seat of Oldham County. It was also the year
Frenchy and Mickey married. With Frenchy giving her name
as Elizabeth McGraw, Scotty Wilson presided as the justice of
the peace and also the bartender. Historians can still see the
McCormick name listed in Scotty's book of marriage licenses.
Apparently they had been one of the saloon couples Scotty,
wanting to raise money to feed his own pocketbook, had
convinced to make their sinful union legal. In *Panhandle
Pilgrimage*, historians Pauline D. Robertson and R.L. Roberston
write, "He called in the dance hall girls and the cowboys and
gamblers with whom they had been living without benefit of
clergy. He impressed upon them a demand to comply with
the new 'law and order.' Among the couples who bought
licenses and were married were Mickey and Frenchy." Marriage must have meant a great deal to the McCormicks, for
they later had the union blessed by a Catholic priest. For the
rest of her life, this marriage license was Frenchy's most
prized possession, taking first place to her trunks filled with
an aging wardrobe.

Mickey may have been a business success in Tascosa, but
he never built his wife a proper house. Elizabeth's (he never
called her Frenchy) home with Mickey was a crude two-room
adobe house that sat on the west side of Atascosa Creek, the

town's namesake. Hardly more than a shack, it was located just about three and one-half blocks from their Main Street livery stable. If she yearned for a real home, no one in Tascosa ever heard of it. The couple lived without electricity, heat, or running water until 1939, when Frenchy finally became too feeble to care for herself.

Mickey made a good living, though. He traveled frequently to deliver passengers or supplies, "...hauling a doctor to Mobeetie or to a distant ranch or was on a hunting trip" report the Robertsons. Like a devoted husband, he sent letters to Elizabeth with every carrier headed for Tascosa. On mail day everyone in town knew that Frenchy's love letter from Mickey had arrived. She always shouted "I heard from Mack!" using her nickname for him. So well known was their devotion to each other that western writers often immortalized their relationship.

Mickey also had a secret past, but Frenchy never talked of it. As an old woman, Frenchy said, "Mack and I discussed the fact that we had lived somewhat on the seamy side, and then he took both my hands in his and we pledged to stick to each other and to the town of Tascosa. And that's what I am to do."

How could they have known that they were pledging allegiance to a town destined to become a ghost. During the McCormick heydays, Tascosa boomed, earning its niche as one of the wildest cow towns in Texas. Down its dirt streets strolled the famous and the infamous, killing and being killed. And because the Canadian River offered easy crossing, Old Tascosa grew to be a thriving den of thieves, gunfighters, comancheros, Indians, and lawmen. Charles Goodnight arrived with the first cattle herd in 1876, and the land boom was really on, with the vice industry taking a lead with its saloons, crooked card games, and "loose" women. One resident once said, "Tascosa thrives on corruption." It was a far cry from that first year the McCormicks spent there when the young town counted only three American women among its Mexican population.

But though Frenchy was one of the first of her kind to settle Tascosa, her name was never listed in local papers as having attended any of the social functions hosted by prominent families. Journalists of her day, however, labeled her as a "respected citizen." The night life gradually lost its luster for Frenchy. She also stayed clear of the seamy element that sprouted roots one-half mile to the east known as Lower Tascosa or Hogtown. Frenchy's neighbors remember her as "someone who looked after me when I was a child."

No sooner had Tascosa begun its life than the death knell began to toll for "Ol' Tascosy." In the late 1800s barbed wire fenced in the town, and the railroad was built on the opposite side of the river. People packed their belongings and moved away, and Mickey was forced to sell his once prosperous livery stable at a great loss. Even gamblers quit coming, and life as the McCormicks knew it began to fade with each setting sun. Progress spread, taming the West.

The money stopped coming, too, but the couple survived. Perhaps man can live on love alone. There was one thing they could depend upon to remain constant—their devotion to each other. Mickey continued to haul and hunt as quail, prairie chicken, turkey, rabbit, deer, antelope, and an occasional buffalo moved in to reclaim what man had tried to take. Mickey took advantage of the bounties ranchers paid to kill coyotes and panthers who preyed on their stock. Frenchy tended to her milk cow, chickens, and vegetable garden, and through the turn of the century, the couple lived on an abundance of provisions. Unfortunately, no children ever came from this happy union, though they loved their hunting dogs and talking parrot.

One day in 1912, Lady Luck turned away for a minute, and death came calling at the McCormicks'. Although Mickey had been quite ill, he headed out the door to go hunting. But, instead of picking up his gun and walking out of the house, the dapper Irishman turned ashen and sprawled across the bed. Alarmed, Frenchy rushed to his side and, according to the Robertsons, said, "He had a strange look in his eyes. I asked him if he wanted water. He said he didn't. Then he looked at me again and said, 'I wonder what you'll do?' I didn't answer. I went to the kitchen. A few moments later I returned. He was dead."

Frenchy buried her beloved husband in a cemetery established by a Spanish settler, Casimiro Romero. From her front yard she could look one-half mile east and gaze on his white marble marker on the hill. Mickey's monument simply reads, "M. McCormick, Feb. 17, 1848 - Oct. 7, 1912." No one from Mickey's family attended the funeral because there was no one to notify. The shroud of mystery that covered Mickey's past lay undisturbed.

The final blow for Tascosa came three years after Mickey's death when the town lost the county seat to nearby Vega. True to her vow to stay with Mickey and Tascosa, Frenchy became the sole resident of a ghost town once known throughout the West as the "Queen of the Panhandle." Deserted and forgotten, Tascosa began to rot away until the stone courthouse stood isolated on streets of weeds and rubble. Harsh weather turned the buildings to skeletons, and the Lady Gay Saloon one day simply collapsed in the dust.

People begged Frenchy to leave the deserted place, but she refused to venture too far away from Mack's tombstone. Worried friends finally left her alone with her memories. Weeks went by without her seeing another human being, and alone she survived blizzards, dust storms, and raging spring Canadian River floods. Even the black Dust Bowl storms of the depression days did not force her to betray her promise to a dead man. Her beloved dogs stayed faithful until they were poisoned one by one by rattlesnakes. Frenchy particularly mourned the loss of Nuggie, her favorite that had become her "ears" when her hearing abandoned her. After Nuggie's death, the result of a venomous bite, friends discovered a den of rattlers that lay coiled and ready under the foundation of her house. She had even killed one that had secretly slithered its way inside the house.

Twenty-seven years went by with the county sending in food, coal, and kerosene once a week. Sometimes, though, the cabin was totally isolated by raging flood water that came from the rising river on one side and creeks on the other. When friends would frequently encourage her to leave, she would shake her head.

Finally in 1939, deaf and failing rapidly, Frenchy reluctantly agreed to leave Tascosa. Her water well had collapsed and the house was crumbling down around her. Before she put one dainty foot in the car, she made her friends solemnly promise once more. "I want your sacred word that if I die away from Tascosa, you'll see that I'm brought back and buried beside my Mack." Then with a weary glance, she looked across to Mickey's grave for the last time before climbing into the car that would take her away.

One Panhandle poet wrote the poem, "Angels Sing of Love Like This."

The shadows grow longer tonight
  In Boothill's lonesome shade,
And Frenchy puts the yearworn light
  By the window, unafraid.

Unafraid that death will intrude
  In her room bleak and old
Where friendly ghosts with manners crude
  Cut cards and ante gold.

Years speed over this grave-crowned hill,
  Still she knows no regret;
But lives on with patient will
  Refusing to forget.

Oh, Death, come quickly to this life
  And cut her bonds, for love
Has won over bitterness and strife
  And Mickey waits above.

She moved to nearby Channing and lived for two more years and two days. During that time Frenchy became a celebrity, and everywhere she went, the press followed. Her time left in the company of loved ones was comfortable for her. She had moved in with a friend, Mrs. Blackwell, and enjoyed the conveniences of the modern world, especially the warm stove, although she never used the electric light. She especially loved sweets and delighted in candied yams. In an interview with the Robertsons, Mrs. Blackwell reported that she would "... bring her a Hershey chocolate bar, and she would smile and say, 'That's what makes me feel so good.'" Mrs. Blackwell explained that Frenchy gained the weight she had lost over the years and grew more active and even kept a pet dog. In spite of her hearing loss and the absence of her teeth, she ate well. She also liked visiting the city, where she went to the movies and watched the Canyon and Dalhert's XIT rodeo. She absorbed the sights in modern Amarillo just as she had when she first set eyes on the rambunctious Tascosa over sixty years before.

Once, the world may have been given a clue to Frenchy's true identity. Two Louisiana women named Charlton saw Frenchy's picture in the Fort Worth paper and became convinced she was their long lost aunt who had run away from Baton Rouge a quarter of a century ago. They begged her to come and live with them, but Frenchy refused their offers with "No one knows who I am, and I'll never tell." On another occasion, she gave a coveted possession away—a rosary she said she used as a young girl. When invited to visit Channing's Catholic church, she decided not to enter the sacred place. Cryptically, she explained, "It might be out of place for me to go into the Lord's house." During the mass, parishioners saw Frenchy as she pressed her face against the window.

Perhaps she saw her own frailties and that is why, in her later years, she distrusted strangers. While staying with Mrs. Blackwell, she secured windows and doors, kept her trunks locked, and slept with her small purse under her pillow. She also covered the mirror with a sheet because she believed the reflection attracted lightning. When she knew the end was near for her, she opened the ancient trunks and gave her cherished clothes to a friend.

At Frenchy's last rites, Father Daley of Channing said, "There may be a foe that can ruin America. It may be infidelity and divorce. In the life of this woman we have a perfect example of love and fidelity. And this should be an inspiration." A marble headstone, erected later, simply read, "(Frenchy) Elizabeth McCormick—August 11, 1852—January 2, 1941."

Some say ghosts haunt the rolling plains dotted with cottonwood trees and etched with the Canadian River and its creeks. Perhaps it's Frenchy McCormick, the "last girl of the golden west," and her man, Mack, as they stand hand-in-hand and gaze over the Tascosa they both loved. It's changed from the town to which they pledged a lifetime. Perhaps they smile as they see Cal Farley's Boys Ranch that is now located here. Whatever their secret pasts, it never mattered, really. All that counts is that their souls are joined forever, their tombstones lit each evening by the setting sun of the Texas Panhandle. As for their dust, it is now part of the land they lovingly called "home."

Note: You can still visit Tascosa as well as the McCormick graves. On a hill nearby is Tascosa's Boot Hill. The cemetery and the courthouse are the only two things left of the original town that made Wild West history. Everything else is gone, including Frenchy's adobe cabin. But as she saw her town disappear with the passing decades, Frenchy once predicted, "Tascosa some day will come back. It's a wonderful town, and people all over the world will know about Tascosa." She was right. Today, Tascosa is alive with 400 boys and girls that make their home at Cal Farley's Boys Ranch, a facility that provides a sound home, school, and work environment for kids in need of guidance. As it is a working ranch, students man the dairy, work the fields, and raise prize stock. Each year on Labor Day weekend, over 10,000 guests come to enjoy the rodeo put on by the school. Since it was started in 1939, more than 5,000 children have grown up there and have gone on to lead productive lives.

As for Tascosa, it's a small, bustling city once again, thanks to the vision of Cal Farley.

ADAH ISAACS MENKEN

The Naked Lady

1835-1868

Paris loved her! London loved her! Havana audiences flocked in record numbers to see their "Queen of the Plaza" perform at the Tacon Theater. She was the toast of such celebrity writers as Walt Whitman, Alexandre Dumas, Rossetti, and the Baroness George Sand. Then came the rumors. All of France was whispering that Napoleon III had fallen under her enchantment and that Empress Eugenie was gripped by jealousy. Even the Prince of Wales followed her career. But who was this Adah Isaacs Menken? Where did she come from? Some believed Adah's birthplace was Chartrain, a village near New Orleans, while others suspected her exotic blood was traceable to Spain. With this most photographed woman of her time, no one could be absolutely sure unless they confided in writer Tom Ochiltree. He not only loved her, but he also grew up with her in Nacogdoches, Texas.

How Adah Menken made it to the Parisian stage of the Gaiete Theatre all the way from Nacogdoches is a study in journalistic savvy. Her meteoric rise to stardom, her baffling personal life, and her ultimate tragic end are all aspects of a tale fraught with myth, perpetuated mostly by Adah herself. Her professional accomplishments that occurred during the Civil War decade are clear, chronicled in both European and American papers. The details of her private world, however, are clouded with a number of marriages coupled with scandals and the constant flow of inconsistencies traced to interviews granted by the actress. Even today, reputable sources relate contradictory data. Such was the enigma of Adah Isaacs Menken, actress *extraordinaire* and aspiring poet who shocked, yet awed, the staunch Victorian world of the mid-nineteenth century.

Historians know that Adah spent her childhood in Nacogdoches and was probably either born there or in New Orleans. Depending upon her mood, she often changed her nationality, vacillating from French to Spanish, Scotch-Irish to Jewish, Creole to Negroid. Her true name, which changed with the seasons, is probably hidden somewhere in Rachel Adah Isaacs, Dolores Adios, Marie Rachel Adelaide de Vere Spenser, Adelaide McCord, or Adah Bertha Theodore. The actress used the last two most frequently when in Texas. When asked about her family's surname, which included a "step-father," she gave either Campbell, Josephs, or McCord. Another story revolves around her father or step-father, James McCord or Joseph Campbell, who probably ran a mercantile or clothing store on the town square near the Old Stone Fort in the 1850s. The 1850 census records are not helpful in solving the puzzle. According to that data, a family by the name of Campbell had daughters in Adah's age range, but old-timers say she went by "Adelaide McCord." Nowhere in the records was there an Adelaide Campbell.

Whatever her true identity, one thing is a given. Adah was a coquette who charmed gentlemen admirers no matter what nationality or walk of life. No one knew this better than her childhood friend Thomas Ochiltree, editor of the *Houston Daily Telegraph*. When he died in 1902, his love for Adah was unfulfilled. Thanks to his writings, though, we have some insight into "The Royal Menken," who was the playmate of kings, princes, poets, and warriors. Tom, also a Texas Ranger and a major in Hood's Texas Brigade, carried the torch throughout his lifetime and did his best to keep intact the image Adah wanted the world to see. After his death, an

Adah Isaacs Menken   (Photo courtesy of the Texas Folklore Society.)

article in the *St. Louis Globe-Democrat* gave a glimpse of the relationship the two shared. Entitled "The Christmas Present Santa Brought to Tom Ochiltree," the piece, signed simply as "Brazos," told of Tom's boyhood crush on Adah when she lived in Nacogdoches with her "docile, illiterate, and unenterprising father and her hauntingly beautiful, educated mother in a log cabin." Even as a teenager, Adah was a strikingly beautiful flirt who commanded the attention of every male who graced her presence. Tom, a carrot-top in his youth, loved Adah from a distance, yet he never had the courage to approach her. He grew to manhood, left Nacogdoches, and joined the Texas Rangers. Returning home from his first Indian fight, he attended a Christmas Eve gathering with other Rangers and friends, Adah among them. She sat enchanted by the story Tom's comrades told of his bravery on the battlefield. That evening a huge banquet and dance took place at the "cuartel," probably the old stone fort that was once used for sheltering troops and providing refuge for women and children during attacks. It was a happy event of gala proportions, and when heavy rains that lay siege on Nacogdoches showed no signs of stopping, the guests decided to stay the night.

Determined to keep the mood festive and hold to Christmas tradition, everyone began hanging up their socks and stockings. Adah urged the timid Tom to do the same. "There's no telling what kind of present you might get," she teased him. Tom hesitated, for he had a particular problem. He had danced holes in his socks, he quietly explained to Captain Rogers. His commander, caught up in the joy of the occasion, ordered him to hang up his boots instead. By Christmas morning, the rains had cleared. On waking, everyone hurried to check their socks for surprises from Santa. Only there was one problem. Tom's boots were missing. Tom suspected Adah was the culprit. Though she had danced mostly with another lieutenant the night before, she had delighted in tantalizing him with coy looks and innuendo.

While others opened little packages and feasted on Christmas delights, Tom tried to look unconcerned. One of his friends said, "If our belle of the ball is not a heartless coquette, I am no judge of women," while another suggested, "Some Mexican must have stolen them." Someone took pity on Tom and gave him slippers. He tried to laugh about the matter, but at breakfast he noticed that Adah was trying to stay in the background. She even avoided his stare. Finally, as she came near, Tom jumped up and shouted, "Now I know what old Santa Claus has brought me. Look at her feet!" Adah had on Tom's boots.

Sometime after that memorable holiday, Adah left Nacogdoches for the big city lights. She kept popping up, however, in such unlikely Texas towns as Livingston and Liberty. Her career began slowly with appearances from 1855 to 1860 in small theaters in Galveston, New Orleans, Shreveport, and Nashville. Her sister, Josephine, performed with her on occasion, although she was not as attractive. Both entertained in Galveston in 1850, where they danced, and Adah stunned a spellbound audience by walking a high wire. Adah claimed she learned the balancing act and horseback riding when she was a twelve-year-old entertainer in New Orleans. Speculation is she may have learned to ride while touring with a circus in early the 1850s. In 1857, after two years of touring the South, appearing scantily clad in Havana and called "Queen of the Plaza," she made her debut in New York at Purdy's Theatre.

In 1855, when her show made it to Liberty, she decided to stay a while. The locals, especially her constant companions *Gazette* editor Henry Shea and lawyer Abner B. Trowel, not only liked her performances, but they also read her poetry. During her six months there, she fraternized with area writers and contributed poems to the local paper, the *Liberty Gazette*. Most of her published work was signed "Ada Bertha Theodore." Adah, though, really wanted to be a dramatic actress and legitimate poet. She entertained residents with Shakespearean readings, but, to her regret, her forte was melodrama. Off stage, she projected herself as the tragic hero-ine. She would rarely smile and puzzled others in her presence with frequent sighs. She was known as a mystery lady whose sadness, some said, stemmed from deep within a bleeding heart. Adah had no female friends but mesmerized male audiences on and off the stage.

When the Civil War erupted, there was little call for actresses. To pay her bills, she read her poetry at coffee houses, published in Hebrew, and consoled herself in Judaic religion she was either born into or adopted through her first husband. All the while, she used the newspapers to create a mystery persona that eventually made her famous the world over. Well known on a smaller scale by 1862, Adah finally hit the big time. On June 3, 1861, in Green Street Theatre, Albany, New York, she opened in *Mazeppa* to a record audience. The show was suddenly the talk of every theater district. In a spectacular scene, Adah made her entrance tied to the back of a wild steed. She, the noble Mazeppa, rode undaunted through a thunderous storm or by treacherous mountains or the threat of a pack of wild wolves. Clothed in Tartar tights and leotard of shimmery flesh tones, the actress's sensual figure seemed nude, covered only by a gossamer drape. Shocked by "the Naked Lady," audiences became enamored by the voluptuous Adah. The role brought her instant fame and fortune as she rode her beautiful horse onto every major stage in the United States and Europe. When Adah opened in April 1864, at London's Astley's Theatre, she was a smash. From there she opened to a packed audience in San Francisco at Maguire's Opera House, where the practice of selling post-cards bearing the star's picture was first introduced. No doubt it was her idea.

In 1866 Adah appeared at the Gaiete Theatre in Paris in a very popular "Les Pirages de la Savanne." Receipts for one week there totaled $70,000. With her career on firm footing, she tried her hand at tragedy by ad-libbing as Lady Macbeth one night in Nashville, where she bombed as a tragedienne. After that, parts were mostly melodramatic with Adah also playing the roles written for male actors. Her sensual figure lent well to male-styled costuming that showed her every curve. Her career continued to soar, and all the while, she was her own staunchest promoter, aware that the pen's power could make or break her.

To ensure that her name stayed in the headlines, Adah relied on her newspaper contacts to cement her name in the minds of audiences everywhere. And if there wasn't anything else to write about, she created incidents. In Baltimore, for instance, Adah made the front page with a dramatic show of support for the Confederacy. Calling herself a "secessionist," she flew Confederate flags from her window until Yankee soldiers arrested her. It was later reported that she so charmed the Union general, he not only released her but he also allowed her to fly her flags. Another story reports that on June 14, 1862, after performing *Mazeppa*, nine Union generals, who were among the audience, were so taken by her beauty that they lost the First Battle of Bull Run one month later.

Adah's tales reached from the believable to the absurd. According to the actress, she once was captured by Indians in the 1850s. According to Adah, it happened when she was buffalo hunting near Port Lavaca. She was captured only to be rescued by Texas Rangers, led by Frederick Harney, who adopted her at age 20 and found a tutor to teach her sculpture and painting. Adah and her tutor fell in love, and angry with the romance, Harney sent her away. In still another laughable version, her adopted father was none other than the Texas hero Sam Houston, who already had a number of children. She couldn't handle the family scene so joined a ballet troupe bound for Mexico. Still another version accounts that an Apache brave renounced his tribe for her. The length of captivity varied from three weeks to three years. From these "experiences," she took with her a riding skill that prepared her for the challenging role as Mazeppa. She had Chief Eagle Eye to thank for teaching her how to ride.

James V. Polk, amateur Texas historian, says Adah lived her entire childhood in Nacogdoches. He was there, he says, and shared it with her. Adah's world, according to Polk, revolved around the town's private schools and the drama club, sponsored by the old Nacogdoches University. Polk says his mother's cousin, Peyton F. Edwards, was also in the organization and encouraged Adah to go on stage. He says she could read and write six languages. In her autobiographical notes, by the way, she listed herself fluent in French, German, Spanish, Latin, Greek, and Hebrew. When it was pointed out to her that the local university offered only Spanish and Hebrew, she replied that she learned them in New Orleans and Cuba. Polk makes additional claims that she was friends with Sir Walter Scott, James Fenimore Cooper, Lord Byron, and Thomas Moore. As Byron was ashes before Adah was born and the others mentioned died before she went on stage, this is unlikely. As none of Adah's names ever appeared on university records, it is curious that Edwards, who was born eleven years later than Adah, ever knew her.

Adah's show toured across the U.S. in 1863 before it played London and Paris in 1864. By that time, Tom Ochiltree had become a respected Confederate hero, Congressman, and journalist. When he was sent to Europe to cover the World's Fair for Horace Greeley and his *New York Tribune*, his path crossed with Adah again. While sitting with his acquaintance, an English nobleman, at a sidewalk cafe, he saw Adah's carriage coming down the boulevard. The nobleman was unaware that Tom had known the famous actress in childhood. "I believe I'll ask A. for a ride," Tom said. His friend was skeptical, betting the writer $1,000 he wouldn't succeed in setting a foot in the carriage. When Tom approached, Adah greeted him warmly and asked him to climb aboard. They rode away, and the next day Tom collected the money.

As for Adah's personal life, a few facts and faces have emerged from the vague world of Adah Isaacs Menken. Records show that in Livingston she married a Jewish musician and millinery salesman, Alexander Isaac Menken, in April of 1856. They met while in Galveston as members of the Neitsch Theatre company of players. Eloping to Livingston, they married April 3, 1856, with Adah signing as her maiden name, Ada B. Theodore. Some reports later place the couple in Liberty, while others say they stayed for a time in Galveston, where Menken engaged in cotton trading during the Civil War. The marriage only survived two years, as Adah made headlines in 1858 by marrying popular New York prize-fighter John C. Heenan without getting a divorce from Menken. When the newspapers got wind that Adah was a bigamist, a worldwide scandal blazed almost engulfing the career of the rising star. Menken promptly divorced her, and Heenan, when he discovered the truth, deserted her, leaving Adah pregnant with a son who died a few weeks after birth.

"Bloodied but unbowed," Adah rose from the ashes to have two affairs, followed by a short-lived marriage to gambler James Barclay, from which a son was born. Adah asked the infamous George Sand (novelist Amandine Dudevant, nee Dupin) to act as godmother to the boy, whose whereabouts are unknown. When the Barclay relationship went sour, another husband emerged in Adah's life. He was Robert Newell, a journalist and satirist who sometimes wrote under the pen name Orpheus C. Kerr, meaning "office seeker." There may have been others; some researchers suspect that Adah may have uttered the words "I do" as many as seven times. Careless about divorces (she remarried twice before divorce papers came through), she also intermingled her marriages with scandalous affairs with such notables as Alexander Dumas and Algernon Swinburne, who vehemently denied it. Recently, someone came to the Sam Houston Regional Library and Research Center in Liberty and claimed to be a descendant of William Henry Harrison Davenport, alleged to have also married Adah. When he learned of her affair with Dumas, Davenport left her and sailed to Australia.

Adah's private life was punctuated by her relationships with some of the most respected writers of classic literature. An aspiring poet whose writings dealt with herself as the victim, she spent much of her spare time with admirers Mark Twain, Walt Whitman, Bret Harte, A.C. Swinburne, Rossetti, and Charles Dickens, to whom she dedicated one of her poetry volumes. Dickens even edited her poetry, which made publication in 1868 under the title *Infelicia*. Though some of her work was good, critics agreed that her poetry lacked immortality. In her poem "Myself," Adah writes:

> *Now I gloss my pale face with laughter,*
> *and sail my voice on with the tide.*
> *Decked in jewels and lace, I laugh beneath*
> *the gas-light's glare, and quaff the purple wine.*
> *But the minor-keyed soul is standing naked*
> *and hungry upon one of Heaven's high hill of light. . .*
> *Shivering in the uprising of some soft wing under*
> *which it may creep, lizard-like, to warmth and rest.*

Galveston's publication *Blake's Semi-Weekly Galveston Bulletin* was not a supporter of Adah, who by the height of her career had become the most photographed woman of her time. One writer accused the international celebrity of hiring well-paid ghostwriters to write poetry for her. *The Bulletin* also chastised her for marrying without the benefit of divorce and of announcing fake divorces to attract public notice. According to some reports, Adah gave birth to several children, often forgetting them when a new man came along.

But Adah was soft-hearted in other ways and suffered financially for it. She spent all her immense fortune on lavish parties and paying off gambling debts for ex-husbands Barclay and Heenan. Always true to her friends, she also gave money to less fortunate actors and actresses and supported charities that appealed to her sense of obligation. Her fledgling career, however, could not take up the slack. In 1867 she tried to replenish her coffers by touring England once again with the legendary *Mazeppa*. Unfortunately, another rival show, patterned after the melodrama, stole Adah's thunder and the chance for a resurgence of her career.

She returned to Paris to begin rehearsal for her other standby swashbuckler, *Les Pirates de la Savanne*. However, her health began to fail, and when a cruel theater manager stormed to her dressing room to demand Adah's presence at the company's first day rehearsal, he found her dead at the age of 33. It was April 1868, and the famed actress who had scandalized and charmed the stiff-necked Victorian audiences took her last breath before two close devotees. A skeptical writer of *Blake's Semi-Weekly Galveston Bulletin* didn't believe she was dead. It's another publicity stunt, he said. But Adah had departed this world, destined to find yet another audience that would marvel as she rode a wild horse through a thunderous storm or understand the full impact of her poetry. She died penniless with all her friends, who deserted her, a safe distance. Only a faithful attending maid and a Jewish rabbi were at her side. Elizabeth Brooks wrote of her in *Prominent Women of Texas*: "She donned her own white bridal robes to meet her last ghostly bridegroom, and thus attired and veiled, was borne to beautiful, peaceful Pere-la-Chaise [cemetery]." Later her remains were moved to the Jewish section of Montparnasse. The grave of "The Royal Menken" is marked with a monolith inscribed, "Adah Isaacs Menken. Born Louisiana, United States of America. Died in Paris, August 10, 1868." On the side of a stone crowned with an urn it says "Thou knowest"—a poignant epitaph considering the many mysteries that surrounded a performer who lived a life of illusion. Yet, Adah saw herself differently. *I am a vagabond, of little use./My body and my soul are in a scramble/And do not fit each other.*

And so, as Shelley would have said, Adah is in her grave, "Half sunk, a shattered visage lies . . ." And yet, the name of Adah Isaacs Menken somehow holds fast to a time when wonder was a wild girl, clad in flesh-colored tights and romantically bound to a huge, black steed, racing into the hearts of audiences from New York to Paris.

EMILY MORGAN

The Yellow Rose of Texas
dates unknown

Some call her a heroine of the Texas Revolution and inspiration for the ancient love song "The Yellow Rose of Texas." Yet, most seventh-grade students who study the Battle of San Jacinto haven't ever heard the name Emily Morgan. It's too bad, as she may have single-handedly caught the great Santa Anna with his silken pants down. Specifics are sketchy concerning her motive, and that lack of evidence has pitted quarreling historians nose to nose. They all agree, however, on one point. An "Emily" was on the battlefield when Houston and his rag-tag band took the Mexicans by surprise, and she was out of sight, concealed in the rococo tent of General Antonio de Santa Anna.

It seems that Emily, a twenty-year-old beauty with finely chiseled features set in flawless "golden" skin, possessed the charm of Cleopatra. Indeed she was capable of taking a man's mind off his duty to God and country. A mulatto, part black and part white, she was gifted—wavy long hair the color of onyx, and dark, beguiling eyes beckoned to every man who saw her.

Most historians feel that she was a slave girl turned indentured servant and a member of the household of Colonel James Morgan, a North Carolina merchant who moved business operations to the new, fertile fields of Texas. To abide by the antislavery law governing a Mexican province, Morgan, who owned 16 slaves, changed their status to indentured servants for 99 years. It was a clever move on his part but slavery all the same. With his partner Lorenzo de Zavala and several New York financiers, Morgan established a town named New Washington on a point of land at the mouth of the San Jacinto River, just a few miles south of present-day Houston. Today it's called Morgan's Point. The businessmen then brought in Scotch highlanders, Bermuda blacks, and other indentured servants to populate the new colony. Emily, a New Yorker who took his surname, was among them. Morgan, probably motivated by the dollar, became a diehard patriot, driven in his support for the Texas cause. He even erected the fortification on the island of Galveston for the protection of refugees and fugitive government officials. He was also wealthy enough to contribute use of his own ships and provisions to the army.

By spring of 1836, emotions raged as Texans, bitter over the defeat at the Alamo and Goliad, yearned to be free from Mexico. As Santa Anna and his men approached southeast Texas, people began to panic. Moving northward en masse to safer ground, these settlers participated in what historians recognize as the Runaway Scrape. This was the case in April as the Mexican forces crossed the Brazos and headed to the capital, Harrisburg. Government officials flooded into New Washington to catch a boat to safety across the bay to Galveston. As the family of President David G. Burnet was crossing in a skiff to board the schooner that would take them across the bay to Galveston Island, the Mexican army appeared on the horizon with muskets pointed. When Colonel Almonte, the officer in command, saw a woman in the small boat, he gave an order not to fire. Here again a woman saved the day—for the Burnets, at any rate. Morgan's warehouse wasn't so lucky. There was no stopping the cavalrymen as they looted stores of whiskey and other supplies, and that night the drunken troops terrorized those left in the settlement of New Washington. The next day, the tired but happy soldiers prepared to move toward the San Jacinto River with their cannon and train of pack mules loaded with provisions and ammunition.

Still gloating from the win at the Alamo, Santa Anna arrived the next day in New Washington, one of the richest provinces in Texas. As usual, he was accompanied by his entourage of fifteen dragoons and 1,000 infantrymen. His mind was on the burning of Harrisburg, an event that made him smile, when his thoughts suddenly shifted. There standing on the dock, helping to load a flatboat, was a strikingly beautiful captive of mulatto blood. He was a man of insatiable appetite—for wine, women, and that ultimate win that would someday put him in Washington D.C. There he would plant the Mexican flag in soil that would be America no more.

Stories vary somewhat as to exact details, but the fact remains that the great general had to have her. He took Emily and a "yellow boy" named Turner as prisoners. Some accounts say that Santa Anna tried to bribe the boy into telling him where Houston and his men were camped. Supposedly, Santa Anna assigned dragoons to the boy to assist him in finding out the army's location. In a clandestine aside, Emily pulled him away from inquiring ears and instructed him to go to Lynchburg where Houston and his army were located along the Buffalo Bayou. He was to tell Houston of enemy approach. Riding a fast horse, Turner slid by Mexican lookouts and warned the Texans on the morning of the twentieth.

At the same time, after sacking every house and burning New Washington to the ground, the Mexican army moved out, hauling "Gold Standard," a twelve-pound cannon. By the time Emily arrived on the plains of San Jacinto with the general, the Texians knew the exact location of their enemy. One account of the battle's eve has a cocky forty-two-year-old Santa Anna aware that he was in clear sight of Houston. Dressed fastidiously in full uniform complete with medals and Napoleon-style headpiece, he paraded in all his glory on a ridge above the encampment. Then, rather than move his men to a better location, the general chose to stay where he was—a spot that left his army open to attack. Motivation for that grievous error was none other than the thought of an undisturbed interlude with Emily—along the banks of romantic San Jacinto Bay.

Probably his thinking processes were also clouded by his opium habit and the lure of the loot he kept in his tent. A connoisseur of great beauty (he loved the luxuries of silk sheets, expensive crystal and silver, and his mounted sterling chamber pot), he foolishly planned to spend the coming evenings, drinking enemy champagne, within the silken partitions of his carpeted, octagonal marquee. Also in the red-striped tent were his opium cabinet, crates of fighting cocks, and a splendid piano.

Adding insult to injury, Santa Anna also underestimated the enemy, erroneously assuming Houston would avoid a force twice his size. Not only did he have a huge army, but General Martín Perfecto de Cós, his cousin, also had just arrived that April 21 morning with 300 reinforcements. Confident, the general instructed them to stack their guns and retire to a nearby rise that was shaded by a post oak grove. Once all were settled for a siesta, he returned to his lavish rococo quarters where Emily waited.

While Santa Anna lounged at his breakfast table where Emily served him, Houston prepared to meet the Mexicans. Early the morning of April 21, Houston ordered Deaf Smith to destroy Vince's Bridge, the only exit to the Brazos River, where Santa Anna's second in command, General Filisola, was encamped. The other bridge, the one Cós and his men had used to reach Santa Anna, was eight miles away. It, too, would have to be destroyed. First Houston sent the scout to the San Jacinto River and a high elevation, to look down onto the Mexican camp and count the tents. From that number, they estimated the number of enemy. Smith not only successfully estimated the number of Mexicans, but to his delight saw hundreds of stacked guns isolated from sleeping soldiers. He also witnessed Mexican officers solely occupied with women in their tents. Houston was aware of the presence of the *soldaderas* and knew that Santa Anna had captured Emily. Smith, from the vantage point of a tree limb, watched as she served the morning meal to the general, who was dressed only in his bright red silk robe. When Smith told Houston about what he had seen, Houston decided to move fast. "I hope that slave girl makes Santa Anna neglect his business," Houston told Smith, "and [he] keeps her in bed all day."

It was a good thing Houston decided to attack, because his men had grown more and more disgruntled. On the verge of mutiny, they couldn't understand why their leader kept retreating. For the past three weeks, he had seemed dulled by the whiskey and frozen in the bottom lands of the Brazos near Groce Plantation. The enemy was closing in on all sides. Houston understood, however, the strategic and geographic advantage of the San Jacinto plains for his small band of Texians. By four o'clock Houston had readied his 783 ragged, yet fervent, men for battle. When all was in place with the Twin Sisters, the Republic's two six-pound cannons, they crawled quietly toward the Mexican camp through the high grass of the San Jacinto plain. Dulled in siesta by drink and the services of the soldaderas, the sleeping Mexicans had no idea of what was about to happen. Their general, too, lay hidden within his rococo tent in Emily's arms.

The Texans were angry and primed for the kill. They wanted blood for that which was shed at the Alamo and Goliad. At four-fifteen, the small band in formation of two men deep and hidden by trees and rising ground, came within firing range. Then twenty paces from the Mexican barricade, Houston waved his hat and led the charge astride his white stallion, Saracen. "Kneel! Shoot low! Fire!" he shouted. Martha Anne Turner in her piece "Emily Morgan: Yellow Rose of Texas" (*Legendary Ladies of Texas*) explains that Houston ". . . continued to caution his men to hold their fire and to aim low. Why did he keep insisting that the men fire only at extremely close range and order them to kneel and shoot low? The answer is obvious: Houston knew that the Mexican targets were *horizontal*, not *vertical*."

Intent on taking no prisoners, the Texians charged, taking the Mexicans by total surprise. The sleepy forces offered no resistance, but the frontiersmen were relentless as they picked off the enemy with little effort. "Remember the Alamo! Remember Goliad!" was their battle call as they avenged the deaths of those who died there. Col. Pedro Delago, Santa Anna's military aide in the Texas campaign, reported, "I saw his Excellency running about in the most excited manner, wringing his hands and unable to give an order." During the deluge, he escaped the pandemonium wearing only red Moroccan house slippers, a linen shirt with diamond studs, and white silk drawers. He hopped a magnificent stallion, Old Whip, who was also a spoil of war, and rode off with only a fine gray vest with gold buttons, a bed sheet, a box of the Harrisburg chocolates, and a gourd half filled with water.

The battle lasted 18 minutes with Houston trying to call a halt to the military massacre. As he himself was wounded in the ankle, it was finally his second-in-command who convinced the Texans to lay down their arms. When the smoke cleared, 630 Mexicans lay dead and 208 wounded. The rest were taken prisoner. The general was later taken prisoner, though at the time of his arrest, his captives didn't realize they had apprehended Santa Anna. Wearing peasant clothes over his diamond studded shirt, he stood before a triumphant Sam Houston. So frazzled was he from the fall of his men and his failed escape attempt, the general had trouble calming his nerves. One account says the general had to chew on opium root before he could conduct himself properly. As the three fifers played "Will You Come to the Bower?" and "The Girl I Left Behind," Texas declared its rightfully won independence from Mexico. One can't help but wonder, however, if the words of the first old English ballad were meant for the general who had been caught in a compromising position with Emily:

Will you come to the bower I have shaded for you?
Our bed shall be roses all spangled with dew.
Will you come to the bower I have shaded for you?
Our bed shall be roses all spangled with dew.
Will you come to the bower I have shaded for you?
Our bed shall be roses all spangled with dew.
Will you, will you, will you, will you come to the bower?
Will you, will you, will you, will you come to the bower?
There under the bower of roses you'll lie
With a blush on your cheek, but a smile in your eye...

Emily told Colonel Morgan about the battle on April 23 when he and Vice President de Zavala stopped at New Washington on their way to the battle site. Their intentions were to provide supplies and reinforcements for Houston's army. Too late to be of any help, Morgan listened intently as his servant told of the Texas victory that had taken place two days before. By that time all the servants of the plantation were buzzing about the news. The story goes that Morgan rewarded Emily for her part in the Battle of San Jacinto by not only granting her freedom but also buying her a Houston home in a community of free Negroes. Later, Emily produced a passport and returned to New York.

Morgan told the story repeatedly. One avid listener was his English friend William Bollaert, an ethnologist, who carefully recorded Emily's story. He was among the first to report the slave girl's account. He kept diaries of what he learned, but for some unknown reason, the extensive *Bollaert Papers* didn't attract any attention until 1902. Then it wasn't until 1956 that a major part of the man's work appeared in *William Bollaert's Texas*. In a footnote, he says: "The Battle of San Jacinto was probably lost to the Mexicans, owing to the influence of a mulatto girl [Emily] belonging to Colonel Morgan, who was closeted in the tent with General Santana [Santa Anna], at the time cry was made, 'the enemy! they come! they come!' and delayed Santana so long that order could not be restored readily again." Another reference is thought to be a clue to the general's romantic interlude with Emily. Bollaert states that Erath believed the victory at San Jacinto was the result of "...Santa Anna's voluptuousness," a term the modern world obviously gives sexual connotation. The story of Emily and her flamboyant captor has been repeated for years by Mexican folklorists. In Mexico, Emily is generally remembered as "Santa Anna's quadroon mistress during the Texas Campaign."

In 1990 columnist Charley Eckhardt gave additional information about Emily. He says she came to Texas from Mississippi with James Morgan and that she went by "Morgan's Emily." "...While her ancestry was questionable," he reports "her beauty—and sex appeal—were not." He goes on to say that the young men of New Washington found Emily irresistible, and that some of the tales regarding their involvement with her are "...outright impossible and others entirely unprintable." According to Eckhardt, some storytellers claim that every male over 16 who lived within 20 miles of the settlement were victims of Emily's alluring spell.

Obviously, at least one great man fell at her feet. But Santa Anna, a pure-blood Spanish Criollo, was always hot-blooded. A "creole," defined as one of pure European ancestry born in the New World, he found dark, sensual women captivating. Yet, what woman could resist his own charms. After all he was Excelencio, Presidente de la Republica de Mejico, Generalisimo y Comandante de los Ejercitios de la Republica de Mejico, Don Antonio Lopez de Santa Ana y Perez de LeBron. (LeBron is the village near the Spanish-French border and home of the great general's mother.) Born in 1794 in Jalapa, Mexico, the "Napoleon of the West" showed great military aptitude at a young age. He grew up brave but reckless, a trait that surely came into play on the afternoon of April 21, 1836.

A world class womanizer caught by his own tragic flaw of passion, the general always seemed to have one thing on his mind. Only recently in San Antonio he had been plotting to gain the favors of a 17-year-old San Antonio girl, Melchora

Iniega Barrera, who lived with her widowed mother. A good Catholic girl, she had refused to give in to the general unless he married her. As Santa Anna had a wife waiting for him in Mexico, he instructed one of his soldiers to pose as a priest and, in a mock wedding, put the girl's mind to rest. Of course, the general made another move out of town when duty called, thereby leaving another conquest in his wake.

The general may have finally met his match when he met Emily. Martha Anne Turner, a former English professor at Sam Houston State University, has authored much about Emily Morgan. She believes the servant was the cause of Santa Anna's insane defense plan that gave Texas the crucial advantage. Historian Henderson Shuffler also called Emily "... the unsung heroine of Texas independence." He says that it is unlikely that Houston's undisciplined band of men could have taken the Mexicans in only 15 minutes without Emily's help. "She had played the Napoleon of the West like Nero played his fiddle, and whilst they had fiddled, a lot more than Rome burned," says Shuffler.

Romantics go on to say that if it weren't for Emily, Texas would have never made statehood. And if that hadn't happened, then possibly New Mexico, Arizona, Nevada, California, Utah, Colorado, Wyoming, Kansas, and Oklahoma wouldn't have either. Shuffler says, "She swapped her questionable virtue for approximately a million square miles of the American West." If only there had been a frontiersman or two who wrote about their experience at San Jacinto, then perhaps the real truth would be known about this intriguing character.

For her part in the Texas Revolution, whether folklore or fact, some believe that Emily, with her yellow complexion, was the inspiration of the famous song "The Yellow Rose of Texas." A few of the words have changed through the years. Originally, these were the first lines of the following verse:

> She's the sweetest rose of color
> This darky ever knew
> Her eyes are bright as diamonds

They sparkle like the dew.
—Original lyrics of *The Yellow Rose of Texas*

The song first appeared as a minstrel song copyrighted in 1853, written by the mysterious "J.K." It later became popular during the Civil War as a marching song for the Texas Brigade commanded by General Nathan Bedford Forrest. The line, "She's the sweetest rose of color" was later changed in the 1940s Roy Rogers movie, *The Yellow Rose of Texas*, to "She's the sweetest little rosebud this cowboy ever knew." Not only did Rogers eliminate the question of racial impropriety, but he also made the song better fit his theme for the "rosebud" made reference to a Mississippi paddle-wheel riverboat.

Some say that Emily as the impetus for the old song is hogwash. They point out that the famous San Jacinto scene is mentioned nowhere in the lyrics and that the Rio Grande which is referred to by the anonymous "J.K." is clear on the other side of the state from the battleground. There will always be skeptics.

It's been over 160 years since the sun set on the rococo tent that opened to the quiet, serene San Jacinto Bay. Yet, the memory of the beautiful and intelligent Emily Morgan lingers. Perhaps the charms of *this* "yellow rose," this *femme fatale* of the Texas Revolution, did affect the boundary of the United States of America. If so, Emily probably never suspected the full impact of her part. Passport records show that she returned to her birthplace, New York, in 1837, never to return to Texas.

The place where Houston and his men surprised slumbering Mexicans with an onslaught of musket fire is peaceful now as it serenely sits beside the flowing river. Tourists picnic near the Twin Sisters and children run through the grove where Santa Anna instructed his men to rest. Towering over the famous site is the San Jacinto monument, an impressive reminder of that fateful day.

As for old-timers, they say that the spirit of a golden-skinned girl comes to San Jacinto every year on its April 21 anniversary to walk again among the oaks that dot the battle-ground. When she is near, some say the scent of roses can be discerned in the soft Gulf breezes. The facts are clouded each year by more and more dissertation, yet the memory of her beauty and her prowess live on.

Margaret S. Henson of Houston, a historical consulate who is a retired University of Houston (Clear Lake) teacher, has written a number of scholarly books on early Texas. She tells of her findings that are contradictory to the much repeated folklore surrounding "the Yellow Rose of Texas":

According to Ms. Henson, Emily was really a free woman named Emily D. West, born in New York, perhaps near Albany. She may have been the daughter of a slave, but she was free by July 4, 1827, when all New York slaves were emancipated. She took her free papers with her when she arrived in a volatile state in December 1835. She left New York City for Galveston on November 2, 1835, with the second wife of Lorenzo de Zavala, Emily West de Zavala, the three Zavala children, and an Irish servant girl on board the schooner, Flash. Part of a group of New York investors who had bought land on the San Jacinto River, agent James Morgan had dispatched the Flash along with the Kosciusko. Both schooners arrived at Morgan's warehouse on the river in mid-December.

Ms. Henson goes on to say that probably Emily lived with Vice President Zavalas and his family on Buffalo Bayou until April 13, 1886. The family stole away to Lynchburg when they heard that the Mexicans were coming. Emily and the other servants stayed at Morgan's place, probably to help President David G. Burnet and his family store their goods in Morgan's warehouse before boarding the Flash, anchored in the river, for a quick escape. With the Mexican army fast on their heels, the Burnets escaped, but Emily was captured. Santa Anna arrived the next day and ". . . perhaps acquired Emily's service." Henson says that Emily probably didn't arrange to have Houston notified of Santa Anna's close proximity. She knew the slave Turner, but she did not know the whereabouts of the Texan army.

On April 21, she, too, managed to escape but lost her free papers in the process. After the battle, Emily asked for help from Isaac N. Moreland because the Burnets and the Zavalas were on Galveston Island, where James Morgan was commander of fortifications. She later went home to Buffalo Bayou with the Zavalas in June because the vice president was terminally ill. After his death, Emily returned to New York in July 1837 with the Zavala widow. Emily never came back to Texas.

Ms. Henson also says that in the nineteenth century, the world "voluptuousness" referred to the general's opium habit rather than his sexual escapades. The facts vary depending on what account you read, but most stories hold to the belief that someone named Emily was present at the Battle of San Jacinto and that she spent two nights with the general in his extravagant three-room tent overlooking the bay.

BONNIE PARKER

Public Enemy No. 1

1910-1934

On April 29, 1934, after returning to her Kansas home from a Sunday afternoon drive, Ruth Warren forgot to pull her keys from the ignition before she climbed out of her stylish new car. As she walked to her front door, she glanced back with admiration at the V8 Deluxe Ford sedan she and her husband, Jesse, had purchased a month before for a pricey $785.92.

Such a beauty, she thought. The soft "Desert Sand" color, fancy upholstery, bumper guards, and a metal cover on the extra tire made her car the most stylish on the block. The distinctive radiator cap was a leaping greyhound in bright shiny chrome. Windows not only rolled up and down but also slid backward two inches. Even the running boards were wide and handsome. "Twenty miles to the gallon!" assured the Topeka salesman, who said the 1934 engine would take them well past the usual speed of 45 miles per hour.

When Ruth later looked out her kitchen window and saw a slow cruising Plymouth coup move past the front of her house, she had no idea the female passenger in the red dress eyeing her new car was the notorious Bonnie Parker. She also failed to recognize Clyde Barrow, the woman's infamous companion. Ruth watched as the coup disappeared around the corner. Suddenly the same car came blazing down the street again, but this time, a young man balanced himself as he stood on the running board. When the coup reached Ruth's drive, the man jumped from the moving car and ran to the new tan sedan. Before Ruth could object, he climbed in, started the engine, and within seconds, the Warren's sleek auto, destined to see 7,500 miles in a reckless twenty-three-day period, was gone.

Those who knew the couple would not have been surprised they picked a Ford. It was a well-known fact that Clyde, a fast and expert driver, always preferred them. He was so enamored with the automobile that he once wrote Henry Ford a fan letter. ". . . Ford has got ever other car skinned," he lauded. Clyde loved the fact that they not only ran at high speeds for long periods without breaking down, but they also burned less gas. And because of their popularity, Fords made the notorious couple less conspicuous on the highway.

It's ironic, then, that this very automobile, later dubbed the "death car," license plate 3-17198, motor number 649198, would carry the famed Bonnie and Clyde to their gruesome end. The Warrens were to see their car again three months later, battered, blood-soaked, and riddled with 167 bullet holes. The right windows were shattered, and the front doors looked like a sieve.

The story of Bonnie Parker and Clyde Barrow began sometime in 1930 at the American Cafe in Dallas next to the old Texas Hotel on Houston Street. Located just a block from the Dallas County Courthouse, the cafe was a popular luncheon spot for courthouse employees, businessmen, and secretaries. Nineteen-year-old Bonnie, who worked at the diner as a waitress, charmed scores of men with her witty sense of humor and good looks. Her reputation for being good-hearted had followed her from the days when she had worked at Marco's Cafe on Main Street, where she frequently served free meals to those jobless from the Great Depression. Already separated for four years from her husband, Roy Thornton, a convict serving a 99-year prison sentence, the freckled-faced Bonnie was determined never to divorce. Once

Bonnie Parker and Clyde Barrow (Photo courtesy of the Texas/Dallas History and Archives Division, Dallas Public Library.)

when she was asked why she didn't make the separation legal, she replied, "It just wouldn't be right."

Of her admirers, two rose above the rest. Later violently pitted against each other, these men would soon play opposite roles in the life of Bonnie Parker. The first was Ted Hinton, who was a young postal employee when he met Bonnie. He would later become a rookie sheriff's deputy and one of the six officers who ambushed Bonnie and Clyde in a rain of automatic rifle, shotgun, and pistol fire on May 23, 1934. Hinton as the last surviving officer of the famous shoot-out wrote *Ambush: The Story of Bonnie and Clyde,* a book that chronicles his two-year manhunt for the couple and the final illegal police trap that ended the lives of the crime figures.

The second admirer was Clyde Barrow. It all started when the dashing Clyde walked into the diner and ordered a cup of coffee. He took one look at Bonnie and decided to make her his woman. Bonnie was attracted to his careless ways, and before long, he convinced her to follow him in his lawless escapades. Before their story came to a bloody end, Bonnie and Clyde went wild in a nine-state crime spree that caused the deaths of twelve people, including nine lawmen.

According to Hinton, Bonnie was not the "cigar-smoking gun moll" the media made her out to be. Rather, she was a petite girl who didn't weigh 100 pounds. A Joplin, Missouri, photographer created the cigar image after he lucked upon an undeveloped roll of film discovered in a room once occupied by Bonnie and Clyde. In one shot, Bonnie is holding a rose between her lips. As a joke, he penned a cigar in its place. The altered photo was copied and recopied so many times, it became a part of the Bonnie mystique. Hinton goes on to say that Bonnie hated the reference to her smoking cigars. She didn't want her public to think of her as a girl who smoked them ". . . because nice girls don't smoke cigars."

Born in Rowena, Texas, in 1910 and educated in West Dallas, Bonnie grew up wanting to be a poet or singer. Hinton describes her as "perky, with good looks and taffy-colored hair that showed a trace of red, and she had some freckles."

And, without a doubt, Bonnie was certainly not the scorned child. She had many friends, and numerous male admirers constantly showered her with gifts. Her popularity, in fact, was astounding. County politicians even asked the attractive young girl to accompany them to political rallies. As for her family, Bonnie was always devoted, and even during her days as a fugitive, Bonnie jeopardized her freedom to secretly visit them. Also, she wrote her mother frequent letters and drove hundreds of miles to mail them. Because of her happy home life, it seemed unlikely she would choose a life of crime. The answer could only be rooted in her love for Clyde Barrow.

Clyde's description is captured in his Texas State Penitentiary file, recorded when he began doing time for burglary and auto theft. The record shows that he was a small man, at five foot, five and one-half inches, with a shoe size of six and a weight of 127 pounds. He wore a heart and dagger tattoo and the initials EBW (for alias, Elvin Williams) on the outer part of his left forearm. A shield with the letters USN was also tattooed on the inner part of his right forearm, though he never served in the Navy. A third tattoo was of a girl's head on the outer side of his arm. Clyde was handsome with brown eyes, fair skin, and chestnut hair, an attribute that probably resulted in his nickname, "Chestnut." Though many didn't believe it, Clyde never drank, smoked, or gambled—with cards, that is. He lived his life on the edge as if events were determined by a role of the dice. He believed alcohol dulled the senses, a luxury that might one day prove fatal.

Clyde hated prison and with the help of Bonnie, who smuggled a gun inside his cell, he soon escaped. He reached Ohio, only to be caught and returned to Texas. Desperate to escape hard labor in the fields, Clyde coerced a fellow prisoner to chop off two of his toes with an ax. He was released in 1932, his papers signed by the governor.

Rehabilitation was never a question for Clyde as he led Bonnie down the road of destruction. Together they orchestrated a string of burglaries, kidnappings, and killings that cast a shadow on even the likes of Machine Gun Kelly and Al

Capone. The pair, joined at different times by W.D. Jones, later Clyde's brother, Buck, and his wife, Blanche, and then Clyde's old buddy, Ray Hamilton, stole greenbacks along with guns and autos, from Texas to Missouri as they moved from one hideout to another. Not only did lack of communication technology in those days hinder their capture, but the pair also had the support of family and friends. Even the newspapers romanticized their crimes, shining a macabre glamour on the pair.

The hometown folks looked at Bonnie and Clyde as just a couple of mischievous kids fighting banks, policemen, and politicians—the forces behind the Great Depression. In *Fugitives*, Emma Krause Parker and Nellie Barrow Cowan try to show that the pair was not all bad. The authors tell that at Christmas 1933, Bonnie went out scouting for toys left unguarded in lawns. She spotted a little car that would be perfect for one of her nephews, and she and Clyde stole it. After a while, Bonnie had second thoughts. "How do you reckon that little kid will feel when he finds his car gone?" she asked Clyde. "I guess pretty bad," he answered. "I'll bet he'll cry. Hell—we'll take it back." The toy was returned without anybody noticing it was gone.

The couple, especially Bonnie, kept in touch with their families as much as possible. Because they knew their phone calls were being monitored, the family used a code known by both the Parkers and the Barrows. When the fugitives were in town, one of the gang members would throw a soda bottle in the Parker yard. Mrs. Parker, pretending to clean up the litter, would take the bottle into the house and remove an enclosed note that stated a time and meeting place. Then Mrs. Parker would call the Barrows and ask if they would care to come over that evening, that she was serving "red beans," a favorite dish of Bonnie's. Once the two families assembled, they would split, then join up again at the secret location. Bonnie and Clyde would be waiting.

Not everybody saw Bonnie and Clyde as just a couple of errant kids. The families of slain officers saw them as merciless killers who shed blood for the thrill of it. During a two-year rampage, the Barrow gang shot their way out of eleven gunfights. Bonnie was hit multiple times, including a wound to her kneecaps, and in a near-fatal car accident, she suffered severe burns, which made her an invalid for months. Things really began to heat up in Joplin, Missouri, on April 13, 1933, when police surrounded a stone bungalow where Bonnie, Clyde, Buck, Blanche, and W.D. were staying. When the siege began, Bonnie, dressed in a negligee, fired repeatedly through the window while the others returned gunfire. Somehow the five fugitives made their way to the garage with bullets flying in all directions and piled into the car. They drove from the melee without a scratch.

Then in July the gang found themselves in another gunfight in Platte City, Missouri. It turned out to be one of the most massive assaults launched by police in United States history. Surrounded by more than twenty law enforcement officers, the five fugitives shot their way to freedom once again. An armored police car, parked in front of the garage to block their escape, was shot to pieces. Four days later, the gang was not so lucky. In a park near Dexter, Iowa, over one hundred men, including police, the National Guard, and local farmers, joined in the battle against the infamous gang. Buck, seriously wounded from the Platte City ambush, took a fatal shot, and his wife, Blanche, suffered an eye wound. She surrendered, but somehow Bonnie, Clyde, and W.D. escaped on foot. Ten days later Buck died in Perry, Iowa. The papers erroneously reported that Bonnie, still recovering from her burns, was mortally injured. Clyde took a bullet in the arm, shattering it. However, it wasn't long before the couple robbed the McMurray Refinery office in Arp, Texas. No wonder the newspapers referred to them as the "Phantom Pair."

"Clyde's name is up, Mama," said Bonnie one evening after Buck's death. "He'll be killed sooner or later because he's never going to give up. I love him and I'm going to be with him till the end. When he dies I want to die anyway." Though police sent word that if she testified against Clyde, she would be set free, Bonnie refused. Clyde even encouraged her to save herself, but she refused. Smitten with the wrong man, love was blind for Bonnie Parker.

The death wagon, in the form of the stolen Ford, would soon claim them on a deserted country road in Gibsland, Louisiana. Hinton learned that the pair had taken on a new member of their gang—Henry Methvin, whose father owned a farm in Arcadia Parish. The trio was visiting the old man at his secluded farm. For two mosquito-infested nights and one humid day, Hinton and his men lay in wait along the gravel road that led to the Methvin farm. With Irvin Methvin as an unwilling decoy (he was handcuffed to a tree while his truck, jacked up with a tire removed, was parked in the road), the hope was that Bonnie and Clyde would see the old man needed help and stop to give assistance. At 9:15 a.m. on Wednesday, May 23, 1934, the Warren's stolen Ford came slowly around the bend. Hidden in the brush and trees, Hinton and the others waited with shotguns ready. Just as the couple came into range, the plan to give them a chance to surrender was aborted. As Officer Alcorn yelled "HALT!" Hinton fired the first shot, beginning a rain of bullets no human could possibly survive. When the smoke cleared, the lawmen had emptied 167 bullets into the tan Ford V-8.

Bonnie and Clyde never knew what hit them. Regaining his composure, Hinton walked cautiously toward the car and then opened the passenger side. He caught Bonnie as she fell toward him. He held her as she gasped her last breath, and he thought of the pretty strawberry blond who had served him coffee so many times at the American Cafe. Hinton noted Bonnie's hat as it lay on the back seat, shot away, and the half-eaten sandwich beside her and the blood-splattered Louisiana map she had been studying. Hinton also noticed Clyde's shoes were removed. He speculated that the jolt of the blast of bullets may have blown off his shoes. He never had a chance to fire his gun.

In a stunning example of overkill, the storm of fire tore the driver's side of the car to shreds. The car lurched forward, rolling down the country road and into a ditch. The ashen bodies of Bonnie and Clyde had each been hit over fifty times. An inventory of the death car showed that along with a shotgun, nine pistols, four Browning automatic rifles, 1,000 rounds of ammunition, clothing, food, and camping equipment, Clyde also carried his saxophone. One rumor that has persisted for years is that Bonnie was pregnant when she died. Autopsy findings show that no pregnancy existed. In fact, Bonnie was not able to have children.

Hinton described the aftermath as people becoming "crazy as loons." The sound of the gun blast brought great crowds from the countryside. Within minutes, men, women, and children were on their hands and knees gathering spent shell casings as souvenirs. Others dug embedded bullets out of trees. Amid the confusion, a wrecker driver hoisted the sedan, and with corpses still inside, pulled it into Arcadia, the parish seat. Along the way people gathered to get a glimpse of Bonnie and Clyde, with a procession of 200 following. When it stopped in front of the schoolhouse, kids flew out to collect a piece of Bonnie's red dress and hair and smear their hands in her blood. One man ghoulishly attempted to whittle off Clyde's ear while the new car's upholstery was ripped apart. By nightfall, a circus quality had taken over the small town of Arcadia, which found itself an unwilling host to 9,000 sightseers. Many could not believe the Phantom Pair was actually dead after all their miraculous escapes.

As a young girl, Bonnie had always wanted to be an actress. The thrill of standing before an audience always stayed with her. Little did she know that on the day of her funeral, an audience of over 40,000 spectators would attend her service at McKamy-Campbell Funeral Home. The largest wreath on Bonnie's casket was placed there by the newsboys. They were, in the end, among the few who had benefited by the short and violent life of Bonnie and Clyde. Since the ambush, the newsboys had sold 490,000 extra papers, about three times their regular sale. Inseparable in life, Bonnie and Clyde were parted in death.

Though it was the wish of the lovers to be buried side-by-side as stated in her poem, Bonnie's mother wouldn't hear of it. "Clyde had her for two years and look what it did to her," Mrs. Emma Parker said. Clyde was buried across town in an unkempt corner of the West Dallas Cemetery next to his brother Buck, with thirty thousand in attendance at Sparkman-Holtz-Brand Chapel. The throng had little respect for the grieving Barrow family and almost pushed the family members into Clyde's open grave. Overhead, someone in a low-flying plane dropped a huge bouquet that landed nearby.

Hinton summed up his account with a curious comment: "We didn't catch 'em. They was never *captured*. They was killed. Once they knew, beyond the shadow of a doubt, that capture could only mean death in the electric chair, they resisted capture, and sometimes by killing their would-be captors. They could continue this way only so long, until they would die. They stuck together, and they loved each other. That just about tells it."

As for the car, Ruth Warren was determined to get it back. She hired a smart lawyer, retrieved the car, and with the gore still on the seats and brains dried on the interior, Ruth drove it to Shreveport and then had it loaded on a van and hauled to Topeka.

Parked in the Warren's driveway again, the car repulsed many of Ruth's neighbors, but she knew just what to do. She leased it to John R. Castle, who exhibited it, and then to Charles Stanley, who bought it. Between 1934 and 1940, many copy cars were seen, but even the fake ones drew big crowds.

Finally, in 1952 Ted Toddy bought the real one for $14,500 and stored it away. When the movie *Bonnie and Clyde* broke box office records, he wheeled the car out of storage and grossed over $1 million exhibiting it. Wouldn't Bonnie and Clyde have been envious? No bank job had ever yielded that kind of money in the 1930s.

All during her manhunt days, Bonnie wrote poetry. It was trite verse, yet perhaps it reveals an unknown softness in a woman gone bad. These childlike lines she wrote are on the

plain metal plaque over her grave in Dallas' Crown Hill
Memorial Park:
"As the flowers are all made sweeter
By the sunshine and the dew,
So this old world is made brighter
By the lives of folks like you."

The Story of Bonnie and Clyde
(Written by Bonnie probably just before she engaged in a
shoot-out with Joplin, Missouri, police April 13, 1933. One
year later Bonnie gave a collection of poems to her mother,
who took them at a secret meeting on an east Dallas County
road.)

You've read the story of Jesse James—
Of how he lived and died;
If you're still in need
Of something to read,
Here's the story of Bonnie and Clyde.

Now Bonnie and Clyde are the Barrow gang.
I'm sure you all have read
How they rob and steal
And those who squeal
Are usually found dying or dead.

There's lots of untruths to these write-ups;
They're not so ruthless as that
Their nature is raw;
They hate all the law—
The stool pigeons, spotters, and rats.

They call them cold-blooded killers;
They say they are heartless and mean;
But I say this with pride,
That I once knew Clyde
When he was honest and upright and clean.

But the laws fooled around,
Kept taking him down
And locking him up in a cell,
    Till he said to me,
    "I'll never be free,
So I'll meet a few of them in hell."

The road was so dimly lighted;
There were no highway signs to guide;
    But they made up their minds
    If all roads were blind,
They wouldn't give up till they died.

The road gets dimmer and dimmer;
Sometimes you can hardly see;
    But it's fight, man to man,
    And do all you can,
For they know they can never be free.

From heart-break some people have suffered;
From weariness some people have died;
    But take it all in all,
    Our troubles are small
Till we get like Bonnie and Clyde.

If a policeman is killed in Dallas,
And they have no clue or guide;
    If they can't find a friend,
    They just wipe their slate clean
And hang it on Bonnie and Clyde.

There's two crimes committed in America
Not accredited to the Barrow mob;
    They had no hand
    In the kidnap demand,
Nor the Kansas City depot job.

A newsboy once said to his buddy;
"I wish old Clyde would get jumped;
        In these awful hard times
        We'd make a few dimes
If five or six cops would get bumped."

The police haven't got the report yet,
But Clyde called me up today;
        He said, "Don't start any fights—
        We aren't working nights—
We're joining the NRA."

From Irving to West Dallas viaduct
Is known as the Great Divide,
        Where the women are kin,
        And the men are men,
And they won't "stool" on Bonnie and Clyde.

If they try to act like citizens
And rent them a nice little flat,
        About the third night
        They're invited to fight
By a sub-gun's rat-tat-tat.

They don't think they're too tough or desperate,
They know that the law always wins;
        They've been shot at before,
        But they do not ignore
That death is the wages of sin.

Some day they'll go down together;
And they'll bury them side by side;
        To few it'll be grief—
        To the law a relief—
But it's death for Bonnie and Clyde.

SOPHIA SUTTONFIELD AUGHINBAUGH COFFEE BUTT PORTER

A Texas Scarlett O'Hara

1815-1897

When Sophia Coffee threw one of her famous parties, everybody, but everybody, came. Even if they had to travel for days by horseback or wagon, no one ever refused an invitation to Sophia's mansion, "Glen Eden." And most of Sophia's guests did have to travel a long way, for Glen Eden was not on a shady street with manicured lawn in Austin or Houston. This gracious mansion overlooked the Red River in the Texas wilderness not far from present-day Denison.

Sophia's husband, Holland Coffee, owned a prosperous trading post near Glen Eden for cowboys driving their herds to the railroad in Kansas. Glen Eden was also popular with dashing young soldiers from nearby army posts, and if Sophia had kept a guest book, in it would be listed such names as Robert E. Lee, Ulysses S. Grant, and Sam Houston.

The Grand Dame of Glen Eden was born on December 3, 1815, in the rough settlement of Fort Wayne, Indiana. Her parents, William and Laura Suttonfield, settled on the frontier outpost because her father, an army officer, was transferred there. Discharged in 1816, the family, including the Suttonfield's seven children, decided to build a log house near a stone building he operated as a trading post. A sutler (supplier) by occupation, William tried his hand at a number of businesses, from mail carrier to the owner of a tavern and hotel, which seconded as a courtroom. He also took an interest in politics and felt right at home in the primitive environment. Apparently, such humble beginnings were not for the imaginative Sophia, who in the coming years described her father as a colonel who commanded Fort Wayne.

Life as a sutler's daughter was not for a smart young girl of Sophia's personality and looks. A stunning, dark-haired beauty, she realized she had no rich future as the wife of a pony soldier, so when she was seventeen, Sophia shook the dust of Indiana from her skirt. Her ticket out of Fort Wayne was the local school teacher, Jesse Augustine Aughinbaugh, who had also been the headmaster of the county seminary. When he heard that Mexico was giving land to settlers, he headed south and took his new wife, Sophia Suttonfield, with him.

By the summer of 1835 the couple had settled in Nacogdoches. Times were tense as Texans grew increasingly tired of Mexico's iron hand. However, once Jesse's entry certificate was secured, he received 4,428.4 acres of land located in present-day Houston County east of the Trinity River. Probably a Pennsylvania German, Aughinbaugh's background was very vague and probably not glamorous enough for haughty Sophia. Perpetuating a dream, she told her friends that it was love at first sight between her and her new husband, and that they had eloped. She also claimed that Aughinbaugh held a high-ranking office in the Prussian army and had left Germany to start a business in Texas. The real facts were probably that Aughinbaugh, proprietor of J.A. Aughinbaugh & Co., druggists, was nothing more than a sutler, just like her father—a man who sold liquor and other goods to soldiers. But Sophia had a way with words.

Somewhere in the first two years of marriage, love between the two must have flown elsewhere, as Aughinbaugh and Sophia parted company. Since the girl was not the type to keep a diary, great blank spaces exist in her life story. Aughin-baugh seems to have vanished with no records emitting a clue to his whereabouts.

To make ends meet, Sophia, known by friends as Sophie, turned to prostitution. Belle Williams, Sophie's companion in later years, said that her friend never spoke of her first marriage but that she said she lived with a band of refugees when she first came to the new territory. Before she knew it, she was running northeast along with every other south Texan in the historic Runaway Scrape, when thousands fled the wrath of Santa Anna and his Mexican army.

By her own account, her story took on a romantic twist. Sophia was the first woman to walk onto the San Jacinto battlefield when the smoke cleared. Not only was she present, but she personally nursed the great Sam Houston back to health. Whether the story has any validity is a matter of conjecture. Jack Maguire in *Legendary Ladies of Texas* theorizes that Sophia may have "...borrowed an idea from her ex-husband and became a sutler of her own. The product she sold, however, was her body and there is reason to suspect that Houston was one of her clients." There is no mention of Sophie in any of Houston's published works, leading to speculation that the hero may have wanted to keep his illicit affair with Sophie from his Baptist friends.

Actually, Sam and Sophia became quite good friends, and later the general visited her at Glen Eden on several occasions. When Sam was president of the Republic of Texas, who should be at Washington-on-the-Brazos, the capital, but Sophia. However, Houston made no moves towards matrimony, and Sophia must have realized her chances were slim of ever becoming the First Lady of Texas. What Houston did instead was place the girl under the care of his friends, Sam and America Lusk. Sam Lusk had fought with Houston at San Jacinto and went on to become an important businessman. Lucky for Sophia that America Coffee Lusk, a descendent of an old Virginia family, had two wealthy brothers. One was to become Sophia's second husband.

Holland Coffee was a great catch. He was a colonel in the Texas army and a new member of the Republic's Third House of Representatives. Not only was he handsome, but he was also old money, two traits that took precedence on Sophia's list of criteria for a mate. Holland was successful in his own right, however, as he owned a string of trading posts where he traded with settler and savage alike. His "Coffee's Trading House," in fact, became the site of several treaty signings, and Indians grew to fear and respect him. It didn't take long for the enterprising Sophia to fall in love. This time she didn't have to fabricate stories about Coffee's brilliant past. He already had one.

Holland was the stuff of romance novels. Fluent in seven tribal dialects, he had an understanding with the Indians and supplied goods to them in exchange for a number of white captives. Mrs. Crawford and her two children, for instance, were traded for 400 yards of calico as well as blankets, beads, and other trade goods. In the case of Mrs. John Horn and her children, Holland failed to convince the Comanche to let the family go free. He tearfully gave her clothing and half of his small amount of flour before he was forced to leave them behind. On the surface, many of his fellow Anglos saw him as an Indian-lover who sold them whiskey and firearms. Even Jim Bowie lodged a complaint about him, saying that he had helped the Indians who raided across the Red River into Texas. Still, the Texas government reimbursed him for ransom expenses.

Aughinbaugh and Sophia had never taken time for a divorce. Determined to make her union with Coffee legal, Sophia took matters into her own hands and petitioned the Harris County District Court to grant her a divorce. When the legal system bogged down, Sophia then petitioned the Texas Legislature, of which Coffee was a member. Finally, after considerable effort and with the help of Sam Houston, the Senate and the House passed a bill granting the divorce on January 15, 1839. Some records show, however, that Coffee and Sophia had already set up housekeeping three years earlier, though a marriage ceremony took place eight months after the divorce.

The happy couple set off to Coffee's Trading Post at Preston in Grayson County. When they finally reached the log trading post on the Red River, a one-hundred-square-foot building resembling a rude fort, the community settlers held a grand ball to welcome the newlyweds. It is hard to imagine just how glittering this soiree was at a remote trading post, but it set the tone for the next fifty years of Sophia's life. She instantly became the society queen of the Red River Valley. Sophie, however, had to pay her dues. She set up their home inside the post and lived there five years with meager furnishings. Her only table was a drygoods box with legs, yet she said she was, "the happiest woman in Texas."

Actually, the post turned out to be a diamond in the rough. Situated on the Red River and near a cut in the bluff that formed a natural chute for herding cattle into the river, it became a great place for cowhands to rest before continuing their way to market. For a social butterfly such as Sophia, it must have been lonesome, though she and Holland attended parties in nearby Warren. All the while, Sophia was making a name for herself as an admired socialite who entertained neighbors and military alike. And when Captain James Bourland's militia company built Bird's Fort (between Fort Worth and Arlington), the troops named a nearby stretch of water Lake Sophia because "it, too, was a heavenly body."

When Coffee announced that he would build her a home, Sophia was probably ecstatic. Now she could really be Queen of the Manor, even if it was out in nowhere. Located down-river one mile from the trading post, Glen Eden probably started as a "dogtrot" two-story oak house of four rooms. The manor also overlooked a bend in the river which invited travelers to visit the Coffees. As years passed, Greek columns, lacy galleried porches, siding, a kitchen, and wine cellar (Coffee was a wine connoisseur) were added. Sophia loved flowers and kept two slaves constantly working to make the gardens a showplace. Orchards graced the back of the house and grape and berry vines covered the grounds to the south. She decorated Glen Eden with expensive furniture hauled by oxen from Jefferson, in those days a major Sabine River port. At last the house was finished, and it was time to show off her masterpiece. One of the finest residences of Red River country, the white Coffee mansion was reminiscent of the great plantations of Louisiana. As for Sophia, she became the reigning hostess of local society.

Through the years, Holland Coffee grew rich in land and cash. Even Sophia acquired land in her own name. It wasn't until Holland was killed that Sophia discovered he owed his brother thousands of dollars for the purchase of more acreage and slaves. In happier days, however, everybody visited the Coffees, from Robert E. Lee to Ulysses S. Grant, as well as other important figures who had a hand in the growth of Texas. Handsome soldiers from the army posts spent many a leisure hour there on the 3,900-acre plantation in the company of Mrs. Coffee, whose social graces hinted of high birth.

Everything went as Sophia planned until she allowed her tragic flaw of pride to upset the apple cart. In the spring of 1846, five years after Holland drew up a will leaving his earthly lot to his "beloved Sophia," he made a codicil to his will. In it, he wrote that extenuating circumstances would probably soon end his life. He was right, for within a few months tensions between him and a relative would erupt into an ugly street brawl. Armed with a bowie knife, a single barrel pistol, a six-shooter, a double barrel shotgun, and a bois d'arc stick, Coffee went after not an army, but only one man— Charles Galloway, his new nephew by marriage. Witnesses say that Coffee went into town and called Galloway out into the street. The polite Charles did what he was told. Suddenly, Coffee knocked him down and attacked him with intent to kill. Galloway pulled a knife and saved himself with three upward mortal strikes. Coffee lay dead in the dirt.

And it was all Sophia's fault. Local folklore has it that Galloway was spreading rumors about Sophie's relationships with other men, including Justice of the Peace Thomas

Murphy as well as the popular Sam Houston. Sophie demanded revenge. She insisted that her husband save her honor and horsewhip Charles. At first, he refused. It just wasn't proper to take an action that would shed light on Sophia's questionable past. With acid tongue, she told him she would rather be the widow of a brave man than the wife of a coward. Pushed to kill, Coffee gave his life so that Sophie's honor could be served. Coffee's demise was a great loss to a community that loved him. As for Charles, who was also a revered citizen, he stood trial and was acquitted. Sophia buried Coffee in a large mausoleum built at Glen Eden by slaves from bricks made on the property. Holland left Sophie with 5,000 acres of land, nineteen slaves, herds of horses and cattle, and his businesses. She also owned several thousand acres in her own name. She also inherited a debt of $2,166 (huge in those days) to her brother-in-law, Thomas Coffee, and he wanted his money. Sophia had to mortgage Glen Eden to settle the obligation.

Sophia mourned her husband's death for a short while, but Glen Eden absorbed her interest with its elaborate gardens and prosperous cotton fields. In spite of lavish parties, the widow heard the call of a city on another shore—New Orleans. On a trip to sell her cotton, Sophie visited the city a year after Holland's death and met her third husband, Major George N. Butt. Sophia did not have to invent a rank for Butt, either. Having left his native Virginia to join the Peters Colony, he was on his way to Texas. A real major in the United States Army, he fell under Sophia's spell and soon found himself manager of Glen Eden. He never did make it to the colony. The relationship was probably a financial one for Sophia. Though Butt was a blue blood, he just didn't look Sophia's type. Arrogant and fastidious, the major nonetheless fit the role perfectly as manager of the manor. A southern bred boy, George brought his love of good manners and warm hospitality to Glen Eden and the beautiful Sophia. George loved parties, too, and he knew his way around the wine cellar. Sophia, however, didn't have it as easy as with Holland.

Sophia Porter and her third husband, George Butt.   (Photo courtesy of the Red River Historical Museum, Sherman Texas.)

George insisted that she, rather than the servants, set the dining room table to his specifications. A smart business man, his worth grew, and by 1850 their combined estate was valued at $18,000. When the Civil War broke out, the sum was $26,000. Five years later, the property tumbled to one third of that.

But happiness was fleeting for Sophia and George, with tragedy striking once again. Trouble started when the notorious Confederate guerrilla leader William C. Quantrill and his gang began spending winters in Grayson County. At first, residents were happy to have the men. Then they began bullying the locals and fighting duels in the streets. One night, Sophie was dancing at a party in Sherman. Suddenly, gunshots rang out, and the tassels on her hat fell to the floor. Two of Quantrill's men had bet that they could shoot off the decoration without harming the wearer. Sophie never missed a step, but George was furious. Heated words followed.

Soon after, in 1863, George went to Sherman, just south of Glen Eden, to sell their cotton. On his way back home, he was ambushed and killed. When Sophie saw one of the guerrillas wearing George's watch, she knew who was responsible for her husband's murder. Sophie rallied the residents and with the help of General Henry M. McCulloch, commander of Bonham's Confederate detachment, and his men, the band was captured. However, Quantrill and some of his men somehow escaped and headed for the lawless safety of the Indian Territory. Sophia returned to Glen Eden in spite of the fact that Indian attacks occurred on a regular basis. At George's death, Sophie was worth $45,400.

Sophia again mourned for a while, but time heals all wounds. Soon Glen Eden was again alive with parties. The Civil War had started, and it was during this period that Sophia became known as the "the Confederate Paul Revere." One day, Confederate Colonel James Bourland and his men, on their way to Fort Washita, stopped by Glen Eden to pay their respects to Sophia. Naturally, Sophia had to have a party in his honor, and it was her usual smashing success. No sooner had Colonel Bourland and his men left the plantation than Union scouts, who were tracking Bourland, arrived on the doorstep of Glen Eden in hot pursuit. Sophia rose magnificently to the occasion. Surely the scouts could rest a bit and enjoy a hot dinner and a little wine. They looked so tired, she convinced them in her sweetest voice. What man could resist Sophia's generosity and hospitality? The Union soldiers took the bait and sat down to a huge feast. After dinner, she invited them to visit her well-stocked wine cellar. Once she persuaded the Yankees to follow her into the dank, dark cellar, she offered them a chance to sample vintage stock. When all had drunk their fill and lay asleep on the floor, the enterprising hostess promptly locked her visitors inside.

Sophia hurriedly saddled her horse, forded the river, and rode to Colonel Bourland with the astounding news that she had captured the enemy. When Bourland's men escorted her back to Glen Eden, they found the scouts sleeping in the wine cellar and took them prisoners, and Sophia became an instant heroine.

The Yankees weren't the only ones who had to look out for the mistress of Glen Eden. When Indians killed a neighbor and threatened to attack her home, she mobilized her slaves and protected the house with a barricade of cotton bales. The Indians stormed the mansion but finally gave up when they discovered they had a worthy opponent in Sophia. The attack of Glen Eden, however, was a turning point for her. Sophia decided life was no party with savages on the loose. Smart enough not to convert all her money into Confederate bonds, she loaded the gold coins that she had on hand into buckets, poured hot tar over them, strung the buckets under her wagon, and headed south to safer ground. Finally she stopped in Waco, two hundred miles from the Red River.

Luckily for Sophia, James Porter was there, too. A member of the cavalry regiment from Missouri, he saw that the Southern cause was lost and was on his way down to Mexico to offer his services to Emperor Maximillian. Once again, Sophia did not have to invent credentials for her new lover. Not only was he a Confederate army officer, but he had also served as judge of the Jackson County Court. Sophia, then 51, and Porter were married in April 1865, by Rufus Burleson, the president of Baylor College. Then she and James returned to her beloved Glen Eden. There they shared a happy twenty-year marriage that ended when Porter died in 1886.

The war took its toll on Sophia's fortune. Her huge investment in slaves went the way of the Confederate bond. But, like Scarlett O'Hara, she still had all that mattered—the land. With James's savvy regarding real estate and a good base of cattle and cotton, their holdings grew and soon their fortune had returned. By 1873 Glen Eden was back to making a fortune for Sophia.

In 1879 Sophie attended the Grayson County Old Settlers Reunion, a gathering for early settlers to share their past. According to the meeting's minutes, Sophie brazenly lied to her old friends. She said she was 60 when, in fact, she was 76. Sophia had always been a woman of great beauty, but age was taking its toll. Expensive fashionable clothes could not bring back her youth and good looks, and she lamented their loss. Mrs. Isabel Skelly Williams, her good friend known as Belle, said she and Sophia constantly shopped to find clothes that would make her look younger. In vain, she ordered dozens of dresses from New Orleans, and Belle also sewed for her. In younger days, Sophia's hair was jet black, a feature suitors found irresistible. Belle faithfully applied Ayer's Hair Dye every week to restore the once-luminous color that was forever "gone with the wind."

Belle was an orphan when she came to live with Sophie after Porter's death. In an interview with the *Sherman Democrat*, Belle told of nights when Sophia would tell her and the servants tales of Indian raids, General Sam Houston, and the Mexican advancement during the Texas Revolution. Too proud to give in to her painful rheumatism, Sophia continued to rule Glen Eden with a firm but loving hand until her death.

Late in life the Porters found religion. Sophie's "conversion" occurred in 1869 when she attended a Sherman revival in which a hellfire-and-brimstone sermon affected her so much that she repented her sins. She gave a convincing demonstration of her conversion to the congregation, crying and shouting as she ran up the aisle and confessing her sins so all could hear. The preacher didn't buy it. He knew of her numerous husbands, her rumored love affairs, and of the many soldiers who stayed in her home for days and nights at a time. He knew of the drinking and the wine cellar. He told her from the pulpit, with the congregation as witness, that "... the sun, the moon and the stars are against your being a Christian." He then told her she would have to serve God twelve years before he would take her into the church. As to be expected, she convinced the preacher to change his mind, and the Porters joined the church in 1869. They showed their dedication to the cause by giving money and land to Sherman's First Methodist Church, including property to Southwestern University at Georgetown. Sophie continued to throw her parties, but dancing was out.

When James Porter died in 1886, Sophia admitted he was the love of her life. For her, his parting took the joy out of the party. So the great hostess gave up her soirees and attended church socials instead. And when Sophia gave her last sigh on August 27, 1897, she was at her home—Glen Eden. She died in her sleep at 81. Four black horses, decorated with black net coats, pulled the hearse. Sophie was dressed in a pink satin dress trimmed with black lace. When she died, her estate was valued at $18,087.17. Her personal property included 14 cows, 46 hogs, mules, horses, a carriage, a sewing machine, tent and wagon sheet, furniture, 5 stands of bees, 25 gallons of wine, 120 pounds of ham, and 143 head of poultry. She left her estate to a niece of Holland Coffee and her faithful overseer, Captain J.H. Williams, who was a Confederate veteran. She is buried near the site of her home with Holland Coffee on one side and James Porter on the other, a fitting arrangement. Scarlett didn't have it so good.

What a life Sophia lived! Although some actual facts are known, what if the walls at Glen Eden could tell their tales!

That can never happen, either. The house was carefully dismantled in the 1940s before the new Lake Texoma flooded Porter's acreage forever. With each board meticulously numbered, plans were to rebuild Glen Eden as a historical site on higher ground. In an ironic stroke of fate, a group of soldiers in training for World War II camped near the carefully stacked boards. It was very cold and dark, and they were freezing. Unaware that the woodpile was indeed the once-majestic Glen Eden, they burned it.

Note: For her outstanding contributions to the development of Texas, Sophia Porter's name was added to the list of Notable American Women, 1607-1950, published under sponsorship of Radcliffe College.

ANNIE STONE MOORE ROTHSCHILD
(Diamond Bessie)
Diamonds Were Not Her Best Friend
1854-1877

The corpse of the beautiful woman lay peacefully in the anteroom of the Marion County Courthouse. Outside hundreds of curious spectators lined up to view the body. As the news of the murder spread, strangers from all over East Texas arrived to see the lady who had fallen from such a dastardly crime. Even gamblers who came to Jefferson to try their luck must have remarked that the mysterious woman, who had once dripped with diamonds, had probably led a hard life. They, too, stopped to pay their respects. Kind citizens of Jefferson passed a hat to pay for the casket, and grave diggers prepared a plot in Jefferson's Oakwood Cemetery to receive one too young and beautiful to go.

The body, which was rapidly decaying, needed quick burial. Two vagrant women performed the highly unpleasant task of preparing it for interment. Then, late on the afternoon of February 7, 1877, Diamond Bessie Moore Rothschild was returned to the earth from which she came. As for the identity of her murderer, he remained a mystery.

The story of Diamond Bessie and her fateful visit to Jefferson began on a warm spring-like day. She and her husband, the presumed "A. Monroe," signed the Brooks House ledger on January 19, 1877. As Jennie Simpson, the chambermaid, led them to their room, she asked, "You all been married long?" The lady blushed, turned her head away, and remained silent. "Two years," brusquely answered the handsome curly-haired man. When Jennie left the guests in the privacy of their room, she heard the man's curses over Bessie's weeping, though she couldn't make out the nature of the disagreement.

That Friday night, the unusually warm weather turned to winter rain. At dinner, "A. Monroe" ignored his striking wife as she sat with a strange fixed smile on her face. Later that same evening, when Jennie passed their room, she heard more crying, then the sounds of violence. The maid wondered how Mr. Monroe could slap and punch his beautiful wife.

The next morning, the couple explored the town of Jefferson but returned sometime before sunset. When Jennie came into their room to fill their lamp, the "Monroes" were resting peacefully on the bed. Sunday morning brought more dreary rain, setting the tone for the crime that was about to happen. Mr. and Mrs. Monroe left the inn again. The woman looked stunning in her elegant black coat trimmed with braid, large buttons, and a silk-fringed hem. Her hair, elaborately coiffed, was topped with a magnificent velvet hat decorated with a white rose and plume. On her hands, large, brilliant diamonds flashed as they captured the light. Even though Mrs. Monroe was a great beauty, admirers found themselves torn between staring at her diamond bedecked hands or her perfect profile.

Dr. J.H. Turner, the Brooks House proprietor, watched them leave. He wasn't worried about the Monroe's unpaid bill because he knew real diamonds when he saw them. Yet, he reflected, there was something strange about the pair. A few things just didn't fit. There was the matter of the heavy trunk that had just been delivered for them. As it sat on the

Diamond Bessie Rothschild. (Photo courtesy of Mrs. Katherine Wise, Jefferson, Texas.)

porch waiting for a strong back to carry it up the steep stairs to their room, Dr. Turner noticed that the canvas cover had slipped. Underneath was a label which read, "A. Moore, New Orleans." If their last name was Moore, why had the gentleman signed, "A. Monroe and wife."

Strangers were a familiar sight in Jefferson, then the largest inland port in the Southwest. Beginning in 1845, steamboat pilots began navigating to northeast Texas from Shreveport through Caddo Lake and Cypress Bayou. The "great raft," a century accumulation of logs and other debris, held back waters of the Red River and Cypress Bayou, allowing the flat bottom steamers to easily reach the river plantation town except in extreme drought. A place of bustling commerce, there were always huge paddle wheelers docked along the busy wharves. Frontiersmen, bankers, merchants, saloon girls, gamblers, farmers, and vacationers alike crowded the lively streets. A port of 30,000 people by 1870, big money, generated from commerce, had arrived in Jefferson. Goods poured in from all over the world, not only for Jefferson's growing flock of millionaires but to be shipped on by wagons to Dallas and Fort Worth.

As the Monroes promenaded Jefferson's streets toward the restaurant where they would have breakfast, townspeople and strangers alike couldn't help but admire the handsome pair. After their meal, the gentleman tried to rent a hack from the livery stable but failed. He then ordered a lunch for two on the pretense of going on a picnic. Resident Frank Malloy saw them as they crossed the main thoroughfare in front of Kate Wood's restaurant. He watched as they strolled into the rising fog that originated from Cypress Bayou. Malloy was the last one to see Diamond Bessie alive.

What actually happened after the fog enveloped the couple, who were later identified as Abe and Bessie Rothschild, is a matter of conjecture. There were certainly no witnesses to the woman's murder. But, Jeffersonians pieced together a likely account of details. They believe that Abe had carefully planned the crime to the last detail. After they crossed the bridge, he chose a private spot, one far enough away so that a gunshot would not be heard in town. They ate lunch and drank beer. The bottle he gave Bessie was probably drugged. When she was unconscious, he took out a pistol, pointed it to her temple, and pulled the trigger, killing not only his wife, but also their unborn child. Abe calmly put the gun back in his pocket, removed Bessie's rings, and with a touch of the bizarre, even straightened her hat. He stretched the limp body out on a large rock and tried to close her staring eyes, but they kept snapping open. Rothschild walked away without looking back at the dead woman who had loved him. He returned across the bridge and back to Jefferson. With the money the diamonds brought him, he could resume his gambling career. Legitimate work was not in the cards for Abe Rothschild, who shunned the dull prospect of going into business with his wealthy father.

Abe spent the rest of that Sunday afternoon chatting with other hotel guests and the proprietor as though nothing had happened. On Monday, the dapper young man walked downstairs wearing two of his wife's diamond rings. When asked about Mrs. Monroe's whereabouts, Abe casually replied that she was visiting friends and would join him the next day. On Tuesday, however, Abe Rothschild vanished from Jefferson.

A freezing winter storm of sleet and snow suddenly hit Jefferson the week of Rothschild's departure. Sixteen days later, the weather finally broke, and Sarah King went to the woods to gather firewood. To her horror, she discovered a woman lying on the wet ground. She walked within six feet of the body, then decided to return to the town to notify authorities. When the coroner, the squire, and the constable arrived, they found Diamond Bessie lying on her back, her head uphill and her hands across her chest. She was still fully clothed and was in a secluded spot fully hidden from the sun. The cold had preserved the body, and the only evidence of decomposition appeared around the head wound. The ashen face was also covered with wood beetles. It was evident that the bullet entering her temple had taken two lives—hers and her baby's. And, there were no diamonds anywhere. The only thing of note that was present at the scene was the remainder of a picnic. Near the body were brown wrapping paper with bread crumbs, a beer bottle, chicken bones, and a few pickles.

It was a good thing that Abe left Jefferson before the body was found. Angry residents would have killed him. In less than two weeks the *Cincinnati Inquirer* was publishing horror stories depicting Abe as a sadistic devil. When the police located him, he was being hospitalized for a self-inflicted bullet wound to his head. Reports say that grief over killing Bessie was not the cause. Rather, he suspected someone constantly following him. So distraught over his suspicions and in a drunken stupor, Abe confided his fears to a bartender late one night. After walking from the bar out onto the sidewalk, he took a pistol from his coat and shot himself, managing only to mutilate one eye and part of his face.

After his recovery, authorities brought Abe back to Jefferson to stand trial in April 1877. Because of legal delays, tempers rose and accusations strengthened against the defendant. On the grounds that the people of Jefferson had became a threatening influence, a change of venue resulted in proceedings being moved to Marshall. Then began one of the first big sensational trials to be held in the state of Texas. Lasting for nearly three years, the trial drew numerous noted lawyers and politicians and set many legal precedents. Charles A. Culberson joined the defense, and Thomas Campbell, the prosecution. Both had been barely admitted to the bar, yet both would later become governors of Texas. Analysts say that publicity resulting from this famous trial put them in office.

The first very brief trial, ending Christmas Eve, 1878, yielded the expected verdict of "guilty of murder in the first degree." Not only was Abe sentenced to hang for the murder of his wife, but he had to pay court costs. The trial was appealed and reversed, and finally a third indictment, handed down in Jefferson on December 2, 1880, yielded a surprise decision. The jury deliberated only four hours, and this time Abe was declared "not guilty." The audience was stunned, and a furor arose. The jury was accused of taking bribes, which could have been true, for the Rothschilds had shelled out thousands to gain acquittal for their son. There was one tale that each juror wound up with a $1,000 bill on the last day of deliberation. Then another story related that each juror received a beautiful piano once the trial was over. A third unsubstantiated tale has each juror experiencing a violent death within a space of a few years following the trial. Though Abe was the black sheep, a Rothschild facing the gallows was unthinkable. Just as the train whistle blew announcing its presence at the Jefferson station, the verdict was pronounced. An exuberant Abe and his parents were whisked outside to a waiting carriage. Within minutes, the Rothschilds were out of Jefferson, leaving behind the memories of the beautiful woman and her unsolved murder.

Annie Stone Rothschild deserved better. Born Annie Stone in 1854 in Syracuse, New York, she was the daughter of a shoe dealer. Her father was a shrewd businessman and family provider. Annie was given the best education money could buy, one far superior to her peers. An aspiring stage actress, Annie also possessed great beauty with black shining hair, flawless ivory skin, and sparkling gray eyes. Her classic features were always accented by fashionable dress.

According to author and retired attorney Traylor Russell, who wrote *The Diamond Bessie Murder and the Rothschild Trials*, a man corrupted Annie Stone. At about age fifteen, she met a disreputable but charming fellow by the name of Moore, also from Syracuse. He used her, then left her, marking her forever as a fallen character. Shunned by her family and friends, she turned to prostitution as her only means of support. She often gave her name as Moore. When her father died, she inherited a considerable amount of money, enabling her to acquire a jewelry box full of exquisite diamonds—those she proudly wore while in Jefferson. Yet, Annie had already tasted the sinful life and had grown to acquire a liking for it. For the next eight years, hers was a life of debauchery. She traveled from

Cincinnati to Arkansas to New Orleans and then back to Cincinnati, where she worked at Frank Wright's "Mansion of Joy."

Then about a year before her death, Annie met a man that would change her life for the worse. While working at a house of prostitution in Hot Springs, she was introduced to Abraham Rothschild, a tall, well-built fellow with extremely handsome features. A womanizer, Abe was the son of a wealthy Cincinnati family, a lineage related to the wealthy banking Rothschilds of Europe. His father, Meyer Rothschild, along with other family members, was prominent in the jewelry business. Abe, however, became an outcast when he turned his back on the lucrative business in lieu of a wilder lifestyle that included gambling and drinking. It didn't matter to Annie. She fell passionately in love with him and hoped their love would reform them both. It was sometime during their affair that Annie became Bessie Rothschild. Whether they made their union legal is questionable. W.H. Ward, editor of *The Twentieth Century*, stated that Rothschild had promised to marry Bessie but kept putting it off. To pay his rising gambling debts, however, he wanted his hands on her diamonds. She would give him anything but her prized jewelry.

Discouraged by Abe's constant delays to marry her, Bessie threatened to tell his father about his broken promise to her. He probably conceived his plan to murder her then. He invited her to take a trip with him to Jefferson. They came through Texarkana on the train and then headed for Linden, where they were supposedly married. No marriage record in Linden could be found, however. It is known that from Linden, they traveled to Jefferson. Speculation is he had planned to kill Bessie before he arrived in Jefferson but never had a chance. Ward goes on to say that Diamond Bessie was pregnant and that was the reason for pressing the marriage. Local Jefferson residents who saw the couple agreed that Bessie looked that way to them.

The union between Annie Stone (Bessie Moore) Rothschild and her man, Abe, was certainly not made in heaven.

One problem was that they both were drunkards, which precipitated constant quarreling. They separated several times during their year together. Abe was abusive and mean, so much so that others had to intervene to save Bessie from his violent temper. On a Cincinnati street one night, the couple engaged in a heated confrontation. A boy witnessed Abe as he shamefully beat Bessie. When the boy tried to stop the man, Abe pulled out a pistol and pointed it at him. Before he pulled the trigger, however, he recognized the child and put the weapon away. Then Abe turned his attention back to Bessie, whom he knocked to the ground. When she got up, they proceeded to the "Mansion of Joy" and rang for admittance. Mrs. Wright, who owned the bordello along with her husband, refused to allow them inside. They then stumbled off into the night.

Funds often ran low for the Rothschilds. While in Cincinnati, Abe took Bessie's diamonds on several occasions, presumably without her permission, and pawned them. He also made her work for him as a prostitute. When the Republican Convention took place in Cincinnati, he forced her to work the streets and give him $50 per day. When she wasn't able to make the quota, he beat her so violently, police jailed him. In the presence of others, Bessie often accused Abe of trying to trick her out of her diamonds.

In December 1876, the couple began their trip down the Ohio River and then south via the Mississippi River. By January they were in New Orleans, where Bessie purchased luggage. She had the pieces labeled with the name, "Annie Moore, New Orleans." The surname "Moore" was one of the names frequently used by the couple, who at times also used their real names. When they arrived in Marshall, Texas, they registered as "A. Rothschild and wife, Cincinnati, Ohio." It was this signature that later gave authorities the clue they needed to track down their murder suspect.

Why they came to Jefferson is anybody's guess, but some believe Abe was in search of a wealthy buyer for Bessie's diamonds. Bessie knew their relationship was rocky, but she loved him. It was her hope that the baby she was carrying could somehow make a difference. All would be well if Abe could just agree to settle down and make an honest living. Bessie hoped that the birth of their baby would prompt her errant husband to return to Cincinnati, embrace the family business, and like the Prodigal Son find his way back into arms of father Meyer.

Abe didn't see it that way. A gambler at heart, he saw the gaming tables as his salvation and was constantly demanding Bessie's diamond rings to finance his endeavors. But Bessie stood firm. She had given him enough. If she gave him the rings, he would lose them as he had lost her diamond pins, bracelets, pendants, earrings, and necklaces that had earned her the nickname of Diamond Bessie. He could mistreat her all he wanted, but she would never give him her last two rings. Therein lay the possible motive for one of the most fascinating crimes in Texas history.

As for Jefferson, known then as the "Queen of the Cypress," it had a chance to guarantee future progress. Jay Gould, railroad magnate, offered the city fathers of Jefferson a chance to become part of his planned Texas and Pacific line. All they had to do was sell him the right-of-way. When they refused, the angry Gould signed the Excelsior House register with the prediction, "End of Jefferson." His omen came to pass. When the great raft was removed, the Red River changed its course, and so did Big Cypress Creek. Boats could come to Jefferson only in time of high water resulting from rainfall. Paddle wheelers no longer unloaded tons of cargo on the wharves. Jefferson lost its influence, and business went elsewhere.

But, because progress never came to Jefferson, today it is one of the best tourist towns in Texas. Everything looks as it did before the Civil War, and most of the homes have been meticulously restored to their original grandeur. The first weekend of May, Jefferson opens its homes to the public for a pilgrimage back in time. One of the most popular events during that celebration is the reenactment of the final trial of

Abe Rothschild. Using local talent, the play has six performances at the Jefferson Playhouse.

Historians say that after the trial, Abe continued to have trouble with the law. That was predictable. Though there is no hard evidence, it's said that he was convicted of a theft against an express company and served 20 years in prison. Another tale has the troubled Rothschild moving to Europe, where he stayed for the rest of his life. As for Diamond Bessie, she still sleeps in Jefferson's Oakwood Cemetery, and her grave is plainly marked.

One afternoon in the 1890s, a handsome, elderly man came to Jefferson and visited Bessie's grave. Some believe it was Abe himself returning to the scene of the crime. He asked Oakwood Cemetery caretaker F.B. Schweers who had paid the burial expense "The citizens of Jefferson," Mr. Schweers replied. The stranger gave the caretaker $10 and then knelt to pray. He then placed a wreath of red roses on the woman's grave. No doubt Bessie would rather have had her diamonds back.

SALLY SKULL

The Two-Gun Terror

dates unknown

Horse trader, champion cusser, trail boss, and wife to many, Sally Skull growled a command and people moved. Her men couldn't decide which was harsher, her black-handled whip or her tongue. They worked from sunup to when the shadows stretched long over the prairie, yet she never cracked a smile. Tough and tireless, this horse woman envied no man. The Confederates owed her, children loved her, her husbands despised her.

Writer John Warren Hunter, father of the noted J. Marvin Hunter of the *Frontier Times,* once wrote of meeting rough and tough Sally Skull: "... I met Sally at Rancho Las Animas near Brownsville ... Superbly mounted, wearing a black dress and sunbonnet, sitting as erect as a cavalry officer, with a six-shooter hanging at her belt, complexion once fair but now swarthy from exposure to the sun and weather, with steel-blue eyes that seemed to penetrate the innermost recesses of the soul—this in brief, is a hasty outline of my visitor—Sally Skull!"

Sally was something of a folk hero in the mid-nineteenth century, and like all heroes, it is difficult to separate reality from the myth. Yet, though many of the records that detailed her life were burned or lost, Sally's unique resolve along with a determination to throw convention to the south Texas winds has prevailed through the years to make her a lasting memory among pioneer stock. A horse trader whose name was known from the Colorado River to Rio Grande, she was a diehard Southerner who by wagon trains freighted cotton to Mexico in exchange for guns, ammunition, medicines, coffee, shoes, clothing, and other goods vital to the Confederacy. A ruthless personality, she ruled her armed trail hands with the crack of a whip and a nasty temper.

No doubt, Sally Skull looked to her own book when it came to rules. When it was unheard of for a woman to ride a horse astride, she did so to the chagrin of female locals. When in the presence of a man, she made herself the dominant force with her strong language that branded her the winning cusser among wranglers. And, she was a flawless shot. Sally could aim over the sight of either of her two six-shooters and hit the target with every try. She loved dancing and draw poker best and was so good with her ever-present whip she could snap flowers clean off their stems. But Sally had one weakness— men. With five husbands notched in her belt, violence seemed to infest her every relationship of the heart. In fact, she may have shot one of them and died at the hands of her last. The details surrounding her own demise would have perplexed even the best sleuth of her day. The old folks told and retold the tale of treachery over and over until an embroidered story is all that is left of the real truth. But one thing was certain. One day soon after the Civil War ended, Sally rode out into the prairie with her fifth and youngest husband, for reasons unknown. At sunset only one rider appeared on the horizon. It was husband number five, Christoph Horsdorff, dubiously called "Horsetrough," *sans* Sally. When asked about his wife, he said she simply disappeared.

As a six-year-old, Sally was among the first Anglo-Americans who settled Austin's colony. She and her family came to the territory with her Pennsylvania grandfather, William Rabb, who was one of Stephen F. Austin's Old Three Hundred. In exchange for his commitment to build a gristmill and sawmill on the Colorado River, he was given virgin land.

Christened Sarah Jane Newman, Sally inherited a strong constitution from her family. She learned early through Rachel, her stout-hearted mother, how to survive in Comanche territory. At times, when it was necessary for husbands to leave wives and children unprotected, the women of Austin's colony, including the Newmans, learned survival tricks early in order to save their scalps from the Indians. The worst and the darkest time was at night when all candles had to be extinguished. One small light meant savages could see through the cabin cracks. Many an uneducated settler had taken an arrow that was aimed through the small slivers.

Cabin entrances were also a problem. In most homes, the door didn't touch the floor, leaving an opening between it and the floor. One day, a band of hostile Indians with intent to kill crept up on the Newman entrance. Rachel, Sally's mother, heard a sound and looked down to see the toes of one intruder sticking under the door. The Indian was trying to raise the door from its hinges. Rachel reached for the ax, raised it above her head, and with a quick, swift motion chopped off the heathen's toes. When other Comanches tried to enter the cabin through the chimney, she set fire to a feather pillow and sent smoke up the chimney.

Sally couldn't have grown up without inheriting some of the Newman intrepidness. Yet, even at an early age, she showed her own courage in the face of danger. Once she watched as two Indians spied on them from the bushes. At the time, she, her sister, and mother were entertaining a neighbor. When the visitor realized that Indians were approaching, his nerve left him, and he pretended his gun was broken. "I wish I was two men," he said feebly, "then I would fight those Indians." "If you were one man," cried Sally, "you would fight them. Give me that gun." The details of whether the child saved the day are unknown, but the image of a spunky little girl standing fearless in the face of danger has lasted through a century of storytelling. The Newmans finally left the unprotected settlement and moved to Egypt, a safer territory, located upriver from present-day Wharton.

Sally grew up with no formal education, which is probably just as well. No teacher would have had the fortitude to deal with such a strong-willed child. But Sally had more common sense in her big toe than most young men her age. Dogmatic and determined, she possessed so much strength that none of her husbands could stand living with her for very long. Her first love affair had all the makings of a storybook romance. The older, valiant Jesse Robinson rode into her life to literally pluck her from the jaws of death. A volunteer in a posse dedicated to the protection of Austin colonists, he and his comrades saved Sally, then a little girl, and her family as almost 200 Waco and Tawakoni Indians threatened to burn them alive. In a frenzy, the band had surrounded the Newman house, eaten some of their livestock, and set fires in the yard throughout the night, when the posse came charging to the rescue.

The volunteers, some of whom later became the famed Texas Rangers, proved themselves heroes. This may have been the first encounter between Sally and Jesse, and though the child was not yet a teenager, she remembered the fearless young man who saved her from a crispy end. The two parted with Jesse joining the Texas cause at San Jacinto. A true hero of the Texas Revolution, Jesse supposedly shot the cannoneer that manned the center of Santa Anna's line. He was present under the shade trees when Santa Anna surrendered to General Sam Houston. He had helped to set Texas free from Mexico's iron rule. In 1836 he went on to serve in Captain Lockhart's spy company of mounted volunteers and continued in service through 1842.

Sometime during 1833, Sally's knight in buckskin came riding back into her life. The two married when she was sixteen years old by the simple signing of a marriage bond, a common practice in early Texas. Five years later, a wedding ceremony joining the two took place and was probably just a legality to cement Jesse's right to land allotted to every married man. Apparently the couple moved to the San Marcos River, which was part of Jesse's parcel of land in DeWitt's colony, and for a while, lived an uneventful life. They had two children, offspring who would bring Sally much joy over the years.

Sally's passions may have been the cause of trouble in their frontier paradise. The marriage began to crumble under the weight of harsh words and betrayal. Jessie finally sued for divorce in 1843, calling his young wife "a great scold, a termagant, and an adulterer." He also named as her lover a man called "Brown." According to the court record, Sally had been harboring and feeding the stranger in an old wash house. How could she have betrayed him, a soldier of the Texas Revolution, he wondered. Jesse also cited her for abandoning him in December 1841 and taking one of their children with her without his permission. Sally countersued, charging that she was a victim of his excessively cruel treatment. Her petition claimed that he wasted her inheritance and asked that the twenty head of cattle and other property she brought into their marriage be returned to her. Both wanted custody of the two children, Nancy, 9, and Alfred, 6. All property was divided equally, but no decision in regard to the children was recorded.

On the boot heels of the divorce, Sally married George H. Scull in 1843. Whether Scull was another skeleton in the wash house is another detail left to the imagination. This marriage, too, was destined for an early grave. Sally must have liked George's last name best, however, because she kept a variation of it through the years. By changing the "c" to a "k," she helped perpetuate an ominous image for herself though George, a gunsmith by trade, was of a gentler nature. A law enforcement volunteer, he served residents of Austin County. He and Sally lived on her strip of land, inherited from her father, near Egypt.

Apparently, bad blood continued to flow between her and Jesse, as nineteen months after the Scull wedding, George and Sally took drastic steps to move from the area. They sold the stock and the last 400 acres of the inheritance, George's prized gun maker's tools and farm equipment, and on Dec. 30, 1844, petitioned for custody of her daughter. With custody refused, the couple abducted both children and headed southeast toward New Orleans. There Sally placed both Nancy and Alfred in a convent where they would get a good education. In a rage, Jesse sniffed out their trail and followed their tracks to Louisiana. Finding the children well taken care of, he pulled them out of the school anyway. But, rather than take them back to Texas, he placed them in another New Orleans convent of his own choosing. Sally promptly pulled them from Jesse's choice and placed them in yet another school. And, so began a tug-of-war that would continue through the children's education.

By 1849 Sally was single again. Nobody knows what really happened to Scull. He vanished from Sally's life without a trace. When asked about her husband's whereabouts, she answered tersely, "He's dead." No one had the nerve to inquire any further. Later around 1853, however, records in northeast Texas surfaced showing George's mark placed on legal papers, signed in northeast Texas. Had George stolen away in the night to escape the wrath of Sally Skull only to turn up far from Egypt? Or was he rotting in a premature grave of which only Sally knew the location? Questions linger.

In 1852 a restless Sally pulled up roots and moved to Nueces County, where she purchased a 150-acre ranch at Banquete, located 20 miles west of Corpus Christi. It was here in south Texas where Sally really began to make a name for herself. There she married John Doyle, who helped her turn Banquete into a trade and ranching center. And it seemed for a while that Sally had finally settled down. Even her close cousin and friendly rival, John Rabb, bought large expanses of land near her and began to run great herds of cattle through the territory.

Sally and her new man shared a mutual friend, jokester W.W. Wright. He and Sally loved to outfox each other and were always dreaming up amusing schemes. Once Sally sold W.W. a horse with a blind eye, a feature John missed when examining the animal. That afternoon, the nag was meandering behind Wright's house when the poor creature stumbled on the underground cistern. The horse plummeted headfirst into the ranch drinking water, where it met a watery death. Wright was left with the huge task of trying to remove the carcass that lay deep down in the cistern, out of reach of normal ranch equipment.

Wright thirsted for revenge. He challenged Sally to a race, a favorite diversion in Banquete. In clear view, Wright paraded his newly acquired horse, Lunanca. Sally knew that the name was Spanish for a horse that is "hipped," or with one hip raised above the other. No fool, she saw this as a chance to take her friend once again. She knew there was no way Lunanca could outrun her mare. She laid down $500, high stakes at the time, and Wright eagerly covered. The town watched as the sad-looking horse hobbled to the starting line. When the shot fired, Lunanca, crazy with excitement, took off like a bullet, leaving Sally's horse in cloud of dust. A seasoned horse trader, Sally had been taken by a mischievous cohort and a second rate horse with bad hips who loved to run.

The fact was Sally knew she could out-trade even the sleekest of crooked coyotes. Usually alone and with big sums of gold in a nosebag draped over her saddle horn, she treaded into stockyards no woman had ever seen before to purchase huge herds of wild mustangs. When her children cautioned her about carrying around so much money, she scoffed at them. And it wasn't unusual for Sally to go alone when taking horses from Mexico to trade along the Gulf coast. Folks in Louisiana saw Sally on a regular basis herding her animals to New Orleans when she had a buyer there.

There were many of Sally's neighbors, though, who suspected that she was a little crooked around the edges herself. They suspected she and her men actually stole stock from her friends. Her *modus operandi* usually involved a friendly visit to neighboring ranches. While she made idle talk indoors with the rancher and his wife, her vaqueros would ride the ranch's pasture lands, cutting barbed wire and running off horses. Local Indians always got the blame. Other critics of Sally Skull said bands of Lipan and Comanche were also on her payroll. Their job was to steal horses and make sure they wound up in Skull herds.

With such a strong business head, Sally really didn't need to steal. When the Civil War broke out, she saw right away that cotton was king. The Union blockade of Southern ports, in an attempt to cut the Confederacy from needed foreign supplies, had stopped ocean traffic between the South and Europe. Cotton meant survival for English mills, and that fact superseded any loyalty on the part of England to the Yankee government. Supply and demand, coupled with international law that forbade blockades from interfering with Mexican commerce, allowed for trade to continue. Texas cotton was simply moved out in ships loaded on the Mexican side of the Rio Grande. In turn, the sale of cotton provided funds for purchase of military supplies shipped into Mexico from Europe. The Camino Real north from Matamoros became the southern anchor of the Cotton Road with Alleyton, the northern point. The Houston railroad line terminated at Alleyton, dropping bales of cotton to be loaded on wagon trains headed to Matamoros. The back haul was lumbering wagons piled high with European guns and ammunition that were shipped throughout the South by rail.

Eager to cash in on turbulent times, Sally dropped the horse trade business for the more lucrative enterprise of running supplies via mule train wagons. Headquartered in Banquete, which was the midway point on the Cotton Road, she kept in her employ a number of desperate Mexicans whom she ruled with a gruff voice. Speaking Spanish with the fluency of a native, she assigned her Mexican crew to take on the duties of wagon train teamsters and began the arduous task of making the switch of goods. Soon she not only became an important figure in the Confederate lifeline, but Sally Skull also helped to nurture a fledgling South.

Everybody recognized Sally as she traversed Texas with her mule train. Although she preferred men's clothes, she wore dresses most of the time. Her favorite attire included a buckskin shirt and jacket and chibarros, long rawhide or coarse cotton bloomers tied at the ankles with draw strings. During the winter, she often wore chibarros of bright red flannel. Sally's grandchildren remember that she sometimes sported a fancy wrap around her riding skirt. Her two ever-present French pistols were always hidden in her skirt when she wasn't sporting her holstered six-shooters.

Sally liked guns and never hesitated to use them. One guilty man found this out the hard way. One year, at Henry Kinney's great fair in Corpus Christi, Sally revealed a darker side. A witness, John S. Ford, tells in his memoirs that as he left the fair and began walking home, he heard pistol fire. Ford raised his eyes just in time to see ". . . a man falling to the ground, and a woman not far from him in the act of lowering a six-shooter. She was a noted character, named Sally Skull. She was famed as a rough fighter, and prudent men did not willingly provoke her in a row. It was understood that she was justifiable in what she did on this occasion; having acted in self defense."

Apparently there were other witnesses as well. A European tourist and author, Julius Froebel, was staying in a Victoria hotel in December 1853 when he heard of the gunfight by others who attended the Kinney Fair. In his journal *Seven Years in Central America, Northern Mexico, and the Far West of the United States*, published in London in 1859, Froebel tells what he heard:

They were speaking of a North American amazon, a perfect female desperado, who from inclination has chosen for her residence the wild border-country on the Rio Grande. She can handle a revolver and bowie-knife like the most reckless and skillful man; she appears at dances (fandangos) thus armed, and has even shot several men at merry-makings. She carries on the trade of a cattle-dealer, and common carrier. She drives wild horses from the prairie to market, and takes her oxen-wagon, alone, through the ill-reputed country between Corpus Christi and the Rio Grande.

Sally was a complex individual with a two-sided personality. Some who knew her say they didn't put it past her to have killed a husband or two, in particular George Scull or John Doyle. Facts are sketchy, but the colorful lore that surrounds the restless horse trader remains. One such tale describes an emotional scene involving an ambush. The husband in question, identity unknown, wanted to rid himself once and for all of his tyrant wife, but she got him first. Another story is that Sally and one of her husbands spent the night in a Corpus Christi hotel after attending a fandango. Having drunk their fill, her man tried to wake her in the morning. Not seeing even as much as an eyelash flutter, he poured a pitcher of water on her head as she lay out cold. Startled but still not conscious of her surroundings, she grabbed her pistol, aimed at her "assailant," pulled the trigger, and killed him—all in record time. Still another surviving version depicts Sally as a wife disgusted with a drunken husband. Catching him as he partook of an open barrel of whiskey, she pushed his head down into the whiskey and said, "There, drink your fill!" Downing his last, he drowned, and Sally wasn't repentant.

Another drowning story flowed around a swollen river. The horsewoman, along with one husband and a group of vaqueros, came upon a tempestuous river while on a freighting trip. The husband walked onto the ferry to stop the ox team and wagon from sliding down the deep bank and into the surging water—only the team kept going, taking the hapless man with them. All fell into the water and drowned. Sally watched as man and beast lost the battle with the raging current at which point she reportedly said with a tinge of regret, "I would have rather seen my best yoke of oxen lost than my man." But when her men asked if she wanted them to retrieve the body, she replied, "I don't give a damn about the body, but I sure would like the $40 in that money belt around it." A variation to the tale describes a fearful husband who would give his life rather than face Sally for losing her team.

With three marriages behind her, she married in December 1855, for the fourth time, to Isaiah Wadkins. After a violent five months, she left him because, according to court records, he beat and dragged her nearly two hundred yards. She also accused him of having other women. When it was proved that he was living openly with a woman by the name of Juanita, not only was Sally granted the divorce, but Isaiah was brought up on charges of adultery. By 1860 Sally, 43 at the time, was living with her fifth husband, Christoph Horsdorff, who was half Sally's age. One old-timer who knew him once said that "Horsetrough" just ". . . wasn't much good, mostly just stood around."

Sally was at the height of her notoriety when she disappeared. Friends knew something was amiss when Horsdorff returned to Banquete alone after he and his wife had taken a ride out of town. "She simply disappeared," said the man, who probably benefited from Sally's estate. Later, a drifter named McDowell reported that as he was traveling over the prairie, he came across the body of a woman buried in a shallow grave. He first spotted it when he saw a boot sticking eerily out of the ground. As the location was desolate, the corpse went unidentified and remained unclaimed except for circling buzzards who marked the spot by targeting their prey. Speculation led to Horsdorff, but there was no evidence.

But Sally had a territory full of enemies. Old records show that Sally faced charges for perjury at one time and was the defendant in a lawsuit, brought by one Jose Maria Garcia. Because the San Patricio County Courthouse was burned, the official reports regarding the cases were lost. However, on one yellowed form relating to the 1867 suit, a cryptic notation was found on one record that said, "death of Defendant suggested."

Frontier mothers who lived in Sally Skull's community loved to threaten their erring children with "You better be good or Sally Skull will get you." Yet, Sally was devoted to her children and on occasion even took neighbor kids with her when she traveled on short trips. Through the years, she was a devoted mother who stayed in close contact with Nancy, her beloved companion, and Alfred, who became a Texas cavalryman during the Civil War. In a letter to his wife, Alfred says that he ran into his mother at King's Ranch. When mentioning the meeting he asks his wife, "Could anyone refer to this two-gun terror as 'mother'?" Yet, Sally Skull would have fought to the death for her children or a close comrade. John Warren Hunter said once, "With all her faults, Sally was never known to betray a friend."

A few dreamers say her adventurous spirit led her to new horizons. Like Elvis, she has been seen everywhere from Goliad to Beeville to El Paso. Or, she may be out there somewhere in a shallow grave—her bones long carried off by animals. Perhaps one day a drifter will find a human skull lying next to a tattered wrap, once fancy, and a tell-tale shred of red flannel, half buried in the sand.

BELLE STARR

The Petticoat Terror

1848-1889

Once a prominent Dallas doctor objected openly to Belle Starr's manner of dress. He objected to her Stetson hat with ostrich plume, her six-shooters worn in a leather holster over velvet dresses, and fringed buckskin outfit with beads that made her look like Buffalo Bill. He just didn't think it was proper for a woman to go riding at breakneck speed through city streets, terrorizing respectable citizens and sending them scattered.

He should have never criticized the notorious Mrs. Starr, who considered herself a new kind of lady. According to researcher P.W. Steele, one day Belle saw the man downtown. "Belle rode up to him, pulled out her pistol, and ordered the doctor to step out of the buggy in front. This put the doctor between the buggy and the horse's rear. When a sizable crowd had gathered, Belle commanded the doctor to grab the horse's tail and raise it up high. 'Now kiss what you see,' Belle ordered him. With a revolver pointing at him, he had no choice but to obey. After the embarrassed man had done so, Belle issued a warning: 'The next time you have complaints about me or my lifestyle, doctor, make them to me.' Then she turned and rode away, leaving a crowd hysterical with laughter. Needless to say, the doctor was never known to ridicule Belle again."

Considered among the most outrageous glamour girls of the Old West, Belle Starr feared no man or beast. She rode through life as fast as her horse, Venus, would carry her, turning always toward the wild side. She made herself a target by living life *her* way but cringed at criticism, no matter how small.

Because Belle was an enigma, and her story, told differently in some fifty books, is a mixed bag of fact and fiction. No doubt she was a "star," a Cleopatra of the plains, whose years on the frontier brightened the seamy side of cowboy kingdom. Unlike the jewel of the Nile, though, Belle hated mirrors. She just couldn't bring herself to look at her own reflection which she described as the face of "a hatchet." Curiously, her homely appearance didn't seem to dampen her love life. A sexually liberated woman with a pleasing figure, dark hair, and bright, intelligent eyes, Belle not only had four husbands, but also a host of lovers, including outlaw Cole Younger and a succession of Indian braves.

Ruthe Winegarten in her chapter on Belle in *Legendary Ladies of Texas* compares the bandit queen to the outrageous George Sand, really Amandine Aurore Lucie Dupin, Baroness Dudevant, Belle's European contemporary. "They both moved in and out of polite society, defying it at will, determined to make their own way in the world. They often dressed as men and enjoyed the free camaraderie of male society. Belle, a crack shot who handled her pistols better than many veteran frontiersmen, complained that all women discuss are pumpkins and babies. Belle and George were small women, olive-skinned, with strong but rather homely faces... They each ran through a long string of lovers, usually younger men, were excellent horsewomen, piano players, and conversationalists." Both also carted their kids off to relatives or boarding schools, and both had daughters who became prostitutes. George's Solange, the highest paid courtesan in Europe, mirrored Belle's Pearl, madam of Fort Smith's finest bawdy house.

Belle Starr and Blue Duck. (Photo courtesy of Archives & Manuscripts Division of the Oklahoma Historical Society.)

The flamboyant Belle definitely affected men whether outlaw or lawman. So what was her secret? In one word— chutzpah. A Fort Smith journalist once said that though Belle had a pleasing appearance, she had a look that was ". . . sure to attract attention of wild and desperate characters." She bowed to no man, and only a fool or a stranger found himself cutting a deal with the calculating Belle Starr. The fact was her business and social practices were unconventional, to say the least, but nobody had the nerve to question her. As for gambling, she loved dice, cards, and roulette and could deal a deck in double-time. As for alcohol, she loved the stuff and had a great capacity to hold it. She loved men, money, and metamorphosis, in that order. She changed husbands as often as she changed her hairstyle.

Belle Starr did not begin life with such a romantic name. She was born Myra Maebelle Shirley on February 5, 1848. Her parents were John Shirley, a native Virginian, known as the honorary "Judge Shirley," and Elizabeth Pennington (Eliza) of Kentucky, a relative to the Hatfields of the McCoy feud. After they married, the Shirleys moved to Kentucky to breed horses and then later relocated to Missouri. The Judge opened a tavern, hotel, and livery stable there, and his place became a meeting ground for Confederate sympathizers and outlaws including Jesse and Frank James, the Younger brothers, the Fishers, and Jim Reed. The Shirleys counted themselves among the many southerners who saw these desperate characters as heroes who promoted the cause by robbing Union banks, trains, and businesses.

Even at an early age and in the presence of questionable characters, young Belle had a nasty temper. A classmate remembers her as a small, dark, intelligent ten-year-old who loved to fight anyone, boy or girl. Belle probably attended Carthage Female Academy, a frontier finishing school, where she learned to play the piano. Belle also loved to sing and dance for her father's clientele who sat for hours at the bar. Frequent visitors to the saloon would occasionally taunt the self-centered and headstrong Belle just to get a reaction. Then an ugly, skinny kid, she would always take the bait, and wranglers would brace themselves for a show of temper unsurpassed in the Ozarks. She eventually learned to channel that emotion, and as a theatrical and self-reliant adult, used it to empower every man she chose.

Apparently Belle's reckless spirit ran in the Shirley family. One brother, Mansfield, met quick death in a gunfight when he was only 15. Another named Cravens, known as "Shug" and later "Doc," mysteriously disappeared, while Ed, a third sibling and known horse thief, was shot to death at age 16. Only Belle's fourth brother, John, affectionately called "Bud," would find nobility in death by giving his life on the battlefield.

Belle's driving personality led her also to do her share in promoting the Confederate cause. A daring horsewoman even at 16, Belle collected information on federal troop movements within Missouri and informed for the Confederacy by riding through the night to deliver facts to William Quantrill, leader of a corrupt army of "freedom" fighters. On the surface, Belle's actions seem heroic, but Quantrill used the information to his advantage. He and his band of bushwhackers pillaged property and murdered citizens who were caught in the chaos of split Missouri and Kansas sympathies. As the question of slavery ripped apart the two states, lawlessness grew to a crescendo when the Civil War broke out. Then neither Federal nor Rebel forces gave residents any peace.

During Belle's underground escapades, many stories circulated of corrupt Yankee soldiers who failed to stop her as she speared through the woods on her steed. A fearless female, she even saved her own brother's life by learning federal troops were set on his capture, though some historians widely dispute this act of nobility. Folklorists say that when a Union soldier finally killed John, Belle demanded to know the identify of the man who pulled the trigger. She vowed to wed any man who killed the low-down Yankee. When she later married outlaw Jim Reed, many thought he had filled her vengeful wish.

When Confederate guerrillas burned Carthage to deny the Union supplies, the family headed to Texas, where they purchased a 464-acre farm at Scyene, ten miles east of Dallas. There they built a home, tavern, and boarding house but failed to make friends and influence the neighbors. Uncaring and clannish, the Shirleys drained the communal well dry, obviously making themselves unpopular in the dry land. Old friends remained loyal, however, as Cole Younger, the Fisher brothers, and Jesse James, along with a host of Confederate refugees, also cropped up in "the promised land."

Texas loved Belle. A popular entertainer at her father's new place, she played the piano and sang her way into the heart of every cowpoke who came to rest his saddle sores. In 1866 the handsome, twenty-four-year-old Cole Younger rode once again into her life. She knew the Youngers from earlier days when the brothers rode beside William Quantrill. Belle fell hard the first time she lay dark, brooding eyes on Cole as he walked through the saloon doors. There was gossip that Belle was pregnant, but the beguiling Cole apparently didn't give a spit. Returning to his gang in Missouri, he left her alone to paddle her way out of an unfortunate situation.

On the rebound, Belle stole away into the night with outlaw Jim Reed. They went to a neighboring town and a justice of the peace married her and Jim, also a member of Quantrill's irregulars. Somehow a *Dallas Morning News* reporter landed an interview with the female bandit. He wrote that she was married in "... the presence of about twenty of her husband's companions. John Fisher, one of the most noted outlaws in the State of Texas, held her horse while the ceremony was being performed, her wedding attire being a black velvet riding habit."

Judge Shirley was livid and refused to recognize the horseback ceremony. According to Shirley descendants, Belle's parents kidnapped her and kept her under guard for some time. Then out of the horizon rode Jim who, like a two-bit knight in shining armor, rescued his dark bride and took her to his home in Rich Hill, Missouri. Rose Pearl was born two years later, and again there was talk that the child's father was Cole, who regularly visited the couple. To add further speculation, when she grew older, Pearl took the last name of Younger. Perhaps Pearl didn't want to use the Reed name because her father's face glared out of wanted posters everywhere. But Belle muddied the waters even more. Probably still holding a torch, she surprised everyone by later

Belle Starr, May 23, 1886. Photo by Roeder, Fort Smith, Arkansas. Photo courtesy of Archives & Manuscripts Division of the Oklahoma Historical Society.

naming the Indian Territory home Younger's Bend. She was married to someone else at the time. That's chutzpah!

With Jim's notoriety a growing threat, Belle returned with her baby to Scyene and the night life of Dallas. It was a good move. Soon Belle was a big name in "Big D." Everybody came to the saloons to hear her play the piano and sit at her gaming table. As for poker and faro, Belle was a shark, and soon she had a wealth of coins and the city of Dallas in her pocket. She loved the bustling cow town, then a wild sinful place alive with crowds brought in with the crossing of two railroads in 1873. Dallas's population suddenly jumped to 7,000, and with herds of longhorns fording the Trinity River, thousands more people poured in from every direction and headed straight for the casinos and saloons. Belle suddenly found herself a celebrity of independent means.

Always a superb horsewoman, Belle next opened a livery stable and dealt in stolen horses. Skies were not that blue for Jim, however. While in Arkansas, he and friends Cole Younger and Frank James became embroiled in the Shannon-Fisher Feud. The whole thing started with a poker game. The Fisher brothers, also good friends of Jim, enticed Maurice Shannon, 16, the son of a successful farmer, to play cards. When the inexperienced boy quickly lost his money, he believed Lady Luck would see him through. He covered the $30 stake by putting in his father's horse and saddle. He lost again, but before he could make the bet good, he explained that he would need the horse to ride home. It and the saddle would be delivered the next day. When he got home, he went straight to his father, Granvill, who became furious his young son had been taken. He angrily confronted the Fishers and threatened to kill them if they ever tried to get Maurice in a game again. As for his horse, he would never give it up. The boy avoided the saloon for weeks but eventually couldn't resist the night life. When he returned in February 1889, the Fishers dragged him into the saloon, stuck the barrel of a pistol into his mouth, and demanded their just due. At that moment, Maurice's brother, Fine, walked through the doors and shot Jim Fisher dead in his boots. The feud commenced with a vengeance and when the smoke cleared, almost a dozen men had bitten the dust. Jim Reed had killed two members of the Shannon party in a general store. After that, every sheriff and bounty hunter west of the Mississippi had his face memorized.

There was nothing else for Jim to do but move again. He and Belle met up again in California, and for a while all was bliss. The law there somehow got wind of Jim's reputation, and the Reeds split again. Jim returned to the Indian Territory, and Belle, along with Pearl and her new son Edwin, took the train back to Dallas where she took up where she left off.

Rumor had it that Belle loved the thrill of the holdup and, disguised, went with Jim on many a heist. On November 20, 1873, Jim, along with Cherokee horse thieves Sam and Tom Starr, stole $30,000 in gold from a wealthy Oklahoma Creek Indian, Walt Grayson, who had lifted the money himself from the Creek tribal fund. Grayson was tortured in the process. One witness reported that one gang member looked like a woman dressed as a man. Belle did show up in Dallas soon after the robbery with a fine string of race horses, including a beautiful black steed which she kept for herself and named Venus. When Reed was later recognized as having partici- pated in a San Antonio/Austin mail coach robbery, things really heated up for Belle, who was also suspect. Jim was soon arrested, only to be released on insufficient evidence. Belle couldn't be implicated for lack of evidence. But she was out- raged. The town gossips just wouldn't leave her alone.

When Judge Shirley was arrested on a trumped-up charge, Belle went wild. She threatened to burn the homes and businesses of those tongue-lashing her family. One night, she and friend Nannie Reed made her threat good. They burned down the store of one woman Belle hated. When Nannie finally admitted guilt, Belle was indicted for arson and forced to pay a $2,500 bail. A friend posted the bond, and for some reason the charges were dropped.

But things had already gotten out of hand. A group of townspeople wrote a letter of complaint to Governor Richard Coke. They asked that some action be taken against Belle for abetting criminals in their God-fearing town. The governor said he didn't have the funds to send a special force down there and suggested that each citizen remain within the confines of the law. Then Belle was charged in August 1875 with stealing a gelding. While in jail, the unstoppable Belle Starr even wove a web around the jailer, convincing him to become her lover and run away with her. Before he could help her, Belle was released for insufficient evidence. As for the jailer, his wife took him back but the town didn't. He lost his job.

Finally Jim's past caught up with him. His life ended abruptly when he was betrayed by a friend wanting the $5,000 bounty. John Morris tricked Jim and shot him while he sat at the lunch table. When he brought Jim's body into McKinney, Texas, to claim the reward, Belle saw through his plot. When asked to identify the corpse of her beloved husband, she answered, "If you want the reward for Jim Reed, you will have to kill Jim Reed. This is not my husband." Morris didn't get his blood money, and Reed was buried in an unmarked grave in a potter's field. A few months later, Morris got his just reward. An unknown assailant shot and killed him.

Belle cared for Jim, but she hated to mourn. Two years later, she married again, but suspiciously this second marriage only lasted three weeks. True only to herself, the Kansas record shows that Belle lied about her real age of 32. She said she was 23. The hapless man was Bruce Younger, Cole's cousin and related to the infamous Dalton gang. An outlaw himself, Bruce's mummified body was discovered in a New Mexico cave. Then three weeks to the day after her marriage to Bruce, a curious tribal marriage record shows Belle tying the knot with Cherokee Sam Starr. The newlyweds moved to Starr's ranch in Indian Territory—Younger's Bend.

A real hot spot, the property became a known outlaw's den under Belle's tutelage. That was because she was the only literate member of the gang, the brain for the band of horse thieves that worked the Texas-Oklahoma border. Horse thievery was big business in the 1870s. Some 100,000 horses were stolen in Texas alone with 750 men the culprits. One day, a slim man with eyes that never seemed to stop blinking came to Younger's Bend. Sam didn't trust him at all, especially when the stranger refused to hang up his guns. "Not to worry," explained Belle. "He's a friend." Sam never knew that the cold, silent man from Missouri was the infamous Jesse James.

Though her actions were less than honorable at Younger's Bend, Belle's neighbors grew to love the female outlaw as a pivotal force at their social events. This was about the time the Honorable Judge Isaac C. Parker took the reins at Fort Smith, Arkansas. Appointed to the bench for the Western District, he was brought in to curtail corruption that had cropped up all over the Indian Territory. He was known as the "Hanging Judge," and his gallows were called the "Gates of Hell." Somehow, Belle endeared herself to the judge. On the surface Belle became an advocate for Indian rights, but actually she stood before the court actively defending a string of known thieves who had all shared her bed. These accomplices, her own partners in crime, were such criminals as Bluford "Blue Duck," Jim French, and Jack Spaniard. She even picked up court fees and hired lawyers to defend them. Dime novelists loved her. They took bits and pieces of her life and glorified the great Belle Starr. To them she became the "Bandit Queen." A showman to the bone, she perpetuated that image by even playing the role of an outlaw in a mock stage robbery at a county fair. The crowd went wild when Judge Parker descended from the coach and at gunpoint handed Belle his watch and money.

The Starrs weren't always lucky, however. In 1883 the pair tangled with the celebrated "Hanging Judge" for stealing two horses found in the Younger's Bend stable. She acted in her own defense in the trial that sealed her fame forever. The judge sent both her and Sam up for one year to the Detroit

House of Correction. While in prison, Belle redeemed herself somewhat by working on a book and tutoring the warden's children in music and French. The first female ever tried for a major crime in Parker's Federal Court, she served six months while Sam stayed a year.

Model prisoners, Sam and Belle returned to Younger's Bend after doing their time. Unfortunately, a violent death was in the cards for Sam as well. On Christmas Eve, 1886, the couple attended a barn dance. Sam saw some men sitting by a campfire and recognized one of them as part of an Indian law posse that had captured him for stealing horses. In the process, Sam's horse had been shot. When Sam asked the man, Frank West, "Why did you have to kill my horse?" both men drew guns, and within seconds each lay dead. Sam, 27, was buried in Younger's Bend.

In no time, Belle was saying the words "I do" again. She practically robbed the cradle when she chose a 24-year-old Creek Indian named Jim July as her fourth thieving husband. The *Dallas Morning News* described July as "... a tall, well formed, Creek Indian with long black hair falling to his shoulders." Belle, who treated him more like a son, coerced him into adding "Starr" to his name. Jim July was certainly up to Belle's standards as an outlaw, and the marshals of Fort Smith were soon looking for him on a larceny charge.

Belle convinced Jim that the marshals had no evidence against him that would stand up in court, so if Jim were smart, he'd turn himself in. She even agreed to ride halfway to Fort Smith with him. On Saturday, Feb. 2, 1889, Belle left with Jim, who was going on to face charges. Belle headed to the King Creek store to settle a $75 bill. Apparently, Belle had a premonition that she was about to meet her fate, as she told the store owner and his wife she feared one of her enemies would try to kill her. Then in an eerie move, she took off her scarf and split it. She gave one half to the merchant's wife as a keepsake. When Belle was returning to Younger's Bend, she was ambushed and shot from behind. A passerby found the dying woman and hurried to tell her daughter Pearl, who arrived just as her mother was about to breathe her last. As she threw her arms around her mother, Belle whispered a few dying words. Pearl never told what they were.

Who killed Belle Starr? The murder was never solved, but folks had their suspicions. That afternoon, Belle had followed the trail toward Younger's Bend that went around the field of a foe, Edgar Watson. Just as she approached the old river road near Watson's hog pen, Belle was shot in the back and tumbled from her horse. The shooter then approached Belle and fired a second charge into the left side of her face. Most feel Watson did it, as the two not only shared bad blood, but also hard evidence pointed to him. Apparently, Watson had badmouthed Belle on many occasions. In an effort to shut him up, she threatened to tell the law what she had heard from his wife—that Watson was a wanted murder suspect in Florida. Another version tells of Watson making advances toward Belle. Angered by her indifference, he killed her.

Other suspects included her son Eddie. A boy who had been in trouble, Eddie was always jealous of the attention his mother rained on his sister. Tensions rose when the teenager asked his mother if she would loan him her prized horse to ride to a barn dance. Because he had mistreated her horses in the past, she said, "No." He took the horse anyway. Knowing that he had to face the music when he arrived home, he stayed gone for a number of days. Finally, he was drunk enough to return home to Younger's Bend. When Belle saw her son, she immediately went to the barn where she found the horse lathered and abused. She grabbed her riding whip and unleashed her rage on her son. He crawled naked from the house and managed to get to the doctor, Jesse Mooney, Jr. "He told his family the story of Eddie Reed coming to him in a very weak condition with deep wounds from a whip all over his body. Dr. Mooney also confided that Eddie said, 'I'm going to kill her for this.'" There were also whisperings about an incestuous relationship between son and mother, a harsh woman sometimes given to sadism.

As a side note, Eddie later redeemed himself, but not until he served time in the pen. Arrested for stealing a horse in the Choctaw Nation, he appeared before Judge Parker. Parker overlooked the lack of evidence and sentenced the nineteen-year-old to seven years in jail. Trying to scare Eddie onto the straight and narrow path, he had made prior arrangements with the warden to have the boy pardoned after only a few months. It worked, as he eventually became a Deputy U.S. Marshal in Fort Smith. He was later fatally shot when he attempted to close a saloon that served poisoned whiskey which killed a man.

As for Belle Shirley Reed Younger Starr, she was buried in the front yard of Younger's Bend. Belle was dressed in her best black silk skirt with a white waist, and in her hand was her favorite six-shooter. The most famous bandit queen in the annals of the West was gone forever. But how the stories linger on! A twenty-five-cent paperback by Richard Fox, publisher of the *National Police Gazette*, came out not long after Belle died and circulated in barbershops, pool halls, bars, and brothels. A treasure of incorrect facts about the Petticoat Terror, it was pure fiction that immortalized the female Jesse James. In the article, the plain-looking Belle became a glamorous heroine, a legend that will always be clouded in doubt. Belle would have been pleased.

Besides scores of books, Belle has been forever frozen in such works as a lengthy 1939 Broadway play, *Missouri Legend*, a 1941 20th Century Fox movie with Gene Tierney, a 1969 London musical with Betty Grable, a 1975 off-Broadway play, *Jesse and the Bandit Queen*, based on a fictional love affair, and a 1980 TV special with Elizabeth Montgomery as Belle. Perhaps people just wanted to think of Belle as a beautiful female Robin Hood, even if they knew better.

This plaintive epitaph is engraved on the tombstone of Belle Shirley Reed Younger Starr. Sculpted by 19th century poet and stonecutter Joseph Dailey, the white marble headstone features carvings of a bell, a star, and a horse—Belle's favorite steed, Venus.

Shed not for her the bitter tear.
Nor give the heart to vain regret.
Tis but the casket that lies here,
The gem that fills it sparkles yet.

Younger's Bend is still there. The Starr cabin is gone, but Belle's land is about twenty miles east of Eufaula, Oklahoma. The ground has been dug and redug many times as treasure hunters look for Belle's gold. Either the bandit queen had an ingenious hiding place, or she had no gold at all because nothing has ever been found. As for Belle Starr, the myth, she, too, remains a mystery.

LIZZIE JOHNSON WILLIAMS
Financial Wizardry on the Cattle Range
1843-1924

"Oh, that poor woman," whispered a lady to her husband as they strolled down Congress Avenue. The man looked up to see a wretched old soul in the distance standing in the shadows of the Brueggerhoff Building. Dressed in an ancient black skirt and faded gray shawl, the woman looked dejected and hungry as she began to walk toward the couple. Moved to charity, the man reached deeply into his pocket and pulled out a handful of change. As the three approached each other, the man offered the money to the pitiful person. She opened a bony hand to accept the gift, and with downcast eyes muttered a "thank you." The woman then turned on her worn heel and quickened her step in the opposite direction. She didn't want them to see the smirk that was forming on her face. *Fools are for the taking,* she thought amused as she headed back toward one of Austin's old-time landmarks and her property—the Brueggerhoff Building.

The emaciated character thought to be homeless was none other than the financial genius Lizzie Johnson. Her Midas touch and eccentric ways were surpassed only by a Texan from another century—the enigmatic Howard Hughes. In an era when a lady wouldn't set a satin slipper in the business world, Lizzie plowed through all corporate barriers. A female financial tycoon, she was nothing short of brilliant—a wizard of a woman who kept her business dealings top secret. Not even her family had a clue to her worth. But Lizzie's investments and schemes, those that made her a millionaire by today's standards, went far beyond the realm of real estate ventures and cattle capital. She had a gift of greenback savvy—insight that yielded mounds of money for a woman who would become one of Austin's best remembered misers.

Lizzie began her road to riches early by hoarding hair ribbons. As a school girl, she kept her own pretty bows tucked in a secret place. It was more practical, she figured, to borrow those of her sister. Everybody recognized Lizzie's brilliance, and at sixteen, she was already a member of her father's faculty at the Johnson Institute, where she taught French, bookkeeping, arithmetic, music, and spelling. There she became a harsh, unrelenting disciplinarian who showed little sympathy for laziness. In fact, her methods were so strict that once the entire community showed their anger after Lizzie levied a severe punishment on a German boy who tried her patience.

Lizzie's father, a missionary turned schoolteacher, was a devout man who battled the bottle. In those days on the lawless frontier, souls were hard to save. It was not uncommon for preachers to find wisdom in whiskey rivers, yet all the while preaching that drink would float a man straight down to the gates of hell. This known vice among men of the Word was just another contradiction found in the Wild West, where laws of moral conduct were written on a daily basis.

The Johnson Institute, a day's wagon ride from Austin, gained a fine reputation as a co-ed school. The first Texas establishment of higher learning west of the Colorado River, it soon became known as a place where God reigned. And no wonder, as it was located far from the big city's madding crowd. Concerned about the temptations of Austin, Johnson turned down an offer of land where the University of Texas now sits. Instead, he chose Hays County as a more appropriate site for his institute. "Old Bristle Top," called by his students because of his wiry pompadour, knew that the

Lizzie Johnson Williams.   (Photo courtesy of Austin History Center, Austin Public Library.)

country would be free of saloon life, a detriment for both students and faculty, himself included. It was a place where students and settlers alike came on Sundays to hear visiting ministers of different denominations preach "fire and brimstone." And when no man of the cloth could accommodate, the Reverend Thomas Johnson himself recited Biblical passages under the live oaks that dotted the campus. With such an imposing father, Lizzie and her five brothers and sisters were sure to take their Presbyterian beliefs to heart.

A proven teacher and student of the Bible, Lizzie decided to move from the Johnson Institute with a chance to teach in Lockhart. Later, she conducted classes in Austin, where every day was begun with a Biblical verse recited from memory. Talented Lizzie also wrote fiction anonymously for *Frank Leslie's Illustrated Weekly* and *Judge Magazine*. With such stories as "The Sister's Secret," "The Haunted House Among the Mountains," and "Lady Inez or The Passion Flower, an American Romance," Lizzie's pen name became widely known. Her true identity, however, remained secret. Money began to flow from her ink pen, and soon she had enough seed money for cattle investments. Parlaying $2,500 worth of stock, Lizzie turned a one-hundred percent profit in three years. Then she sold it for $20,000, materializing her gain into land and more cattle. Travis County records, dated 1871, show the registration of her CY brand, marking her arrival as an equal among cattle dealers.

How she became so shrewd about the cattle business probably had something to do with the fact that she kept books for many of the successful area cattlemen. One tale about Lizzie exemplifies this strange relationship she had with her male counterparts. As a businesswoman, Lizzie had a number of dealings with a man named Major George W. Littlefield. The major later became well respected as the founder and president of American National Bank. When Lizzie, well into her seventies, ventured into Austin, she would see Littlefield on the street. "Hello, you old cattle thief!" she always called. The polite businessman would simply bow and smile. It was a known fact that only proven cattlemen had the privilege of speaking to each other in this fashion.

Prosperity breeds confidence, and as Lizzie's herds grew, so did her reputation as a dispassionate businesswoman. Her exterior, though, was deceiving. Pictures of Lizzie show a girl of slender build and medium height with thick dark hair worn up most of the time. In her younger days, her hairstyle, with bangs and two long curls at the nape of the neck, was her trademark. She was no raving beauty but was considered attractive by that day's standards. Her clothes, though, not only gave her a mark of distinction, but she also used them to create illusions. Her hats, for instance, added height. Hotel employees always had warning when the fashionable Miss Johnson came their way. They could see her slender plumed chapeau, always secured with its expensive jeweled pin, pointing up over the crowd gathered in the lobby. Lizzie also considered herself a fashion setter. When buying scores of silk and satin dresses, the frugal Miss Johnson never batted an eye when she looked at the price tag. As for her closet, it was crowded with rows of high-buttoned shoes for daytime and spool-heeled slippers for night. And when her attire lacked flowers, it had feathers. In her wedding picture, she sports a skirt that stood out around her toes like an elongated bell, giving an air of total femininity—a laughable illusion for one so dogmatic. Her early dresses, still owned by Mrs. John E. Shelton, a niece, show a tiny waistline of eighteen inches. One saved creation is a black bustled sateen trimmed with black lace and jet beads. Another is gold with ruffles at the hem and trimmed with lace.

In her youth, Lizzie dressed like a lady and did business like a man. She didn't like to socialize and chose to keep her private and professional affairs quiet. In fact, not even her family had a clue about her business. Once her brother showed interest in buying a building in Austin, and upon inquiry, found out to his total surprise that it belonged to his sister.

Lizzie was a Southerner, but she didn't see any reason why a person shouldn't benefit from the Civil War. Life as Texans knew it had come to a screeching halt by 1860. Men left their families and farms to fight for the Confederate cause, and with that exodus, chaos reigned supreme in most communities. With so many men on the battleground and slaves along to tend their masters, stock crossed broken fences and roamed free. As the years passed, unclaimed herds trampled the plains, and calves, increasing the population at twenty-five percent a year, went unbranded. When the Reconstruction era followed, it brought more disorder. Mexican ranchers, for example, decided life was sweeter after all on the other side of the border. Leaving more land and cattle up for grabs, they deserted their investments and headed south away from the intruding Yankee. According to the *Southwestern Historical Quarterly*, the "skinning war" then commenced. As cattle prices tumbled, thousands of animals were slaughtered for hide and tallow. Buzzards, filling the skies, preyed on what was left.

When the war ended in 1865, however, the Yankee was starving for Texas beef. Northern prices soared to ten times as much as in Texas. All along, Lizzie had been "brush-popping," the act of flushing out wandering longhorns into her waiting arms. She claimed the steers as her own, guiding them into her growing herds. A well-known fact about Lizzie was that she knew her cows. Old-timers told how when Lizzie came to the stockyards to buy cattle, she would stand by a chute all day long pointing out the head she wanted.

When Lizzie was thirty-six, she shocked everybody and decided to get married. Her strange choice of a mate was Hezekiah Williams, a rancher cum preacher who was also fond of hard liquor. Despite Hezekiah's charm, Lizzie was no dummy. She watched her new husband with calculating eyes. Soon she learned that though Hezekiah was a handsome widower with flowing mustache and full beard, he just didn't have good business sense. Even though she loved Hezekiah, she did not trust his financial acumen. Unheard of in those days, the astute Lizzie had Hezekiah, the father of several children by a previous marriage, sign a prenuptial agreement that her property and profits remained totally hers forever.

As time passed, Hezekiah and Lizzie often bought from the same herd at the same time, but each handled his and her steers separately. Lizzie, who always banked hefty profits, customarily bought then sold the same cattle in the same day. Hezekiah, on the other hand, was the gambler. He liked to hold on to his herd for a better price that never came. He not only lost money on a regular basis but never learned from his mistakes. Lucky for him, Lizzie always bailed him out, sometimes shelling out as much as $50,000 to get him back on his feet. He was always required to sign a note, however, and was expected to pay back every nickel. And, even though she probably charged him interest, Lizzie was devoted to him.

Hezekiah recorded his own brand on August 13, 1881, two years after their marriage and a little more than ten years after Lizzie recorded hers. When the time came to drive the collective herds to the Kansas City market, Lizzie did an incredible thing—she went along, too. There was no way she could trust a man with Hezekiah's weaknesses to supervise a long, dangerous cattle drive up the Chisholm Trail, plagued by hostile Indians. In the history of trail driving, Lizzie then became one of only three cattle queens (the others are Amanda Burks and Mary Taylor Bunton) who followed the famous trail in the late 1800s.

Hezekiah and Lizzie journeyed as husband and wife, but they also made the trip as independent cattlemen. Cowhands kept herds strictly separate all the way, and the only common thing the Williams shared was a foreman. On the sly, Lizzie would call the man aside and order him to use her brand to mark any unbranded longhorns that belonged to Hezekiah. In an amusing twist, Hezekiah gave the frazzled foreman similar instructions, only he was to claim as Hezekiah's all of Lizzie's brandless head.

Riding behind the herd in a strong sturdy buggy, Lizzie made the dangerous journey without complaint. She had a big investment at stake, and complaining was never in her nature. She adored fancy clothes, but for the Chisholm Trail, it was a calico dress, layers of heavy petticoats, and a dowdy sunbonnet to protect her skin. On the trail, Lizzie truly found her element—she loved the rough world of the range, too dangerous for the slight-of-heart. Her wranglers liked her spunky spirit and lavished her with gifts of wild fruit, prairie chicken, and antelope's tongue. But though she preferred the company of cowboys, she always maintained the manners of a Southern lady. This indomitable woman made the trip several times between the years 1879 and 1889, always with a successful drive. Because she turned her back on the traditional female roles of the day, Lizzie was looked upon all her life as somewhat odd—sometimes even downright mean. The fact was this cattle queen much preferred the cowpoke to the bank president.

By 1890 the big cattle boom was over, but it didn't matter because Lizzie had made a fortune. Another venture tantalized her financial psyche—the lure of real estate. Her first purchase was the Brueggerhoff Building on Congress Avenue in Austin, and from there she went on to buy up city lots and buildings. When she died in 1924, her real estate holdings were estimated at $164,339. Owner of one of the largest fortunes in Texas in her day, Lizzie never asked for advice—it might have dampened her financial wizardry.

Together, Lizzie and Hezekiah did own one piece of property, the Williams Ranch of several thousand acres near Driftwood in Hays County. They organized a town called Hays City which had only two streets. One was Johnson Street for Lizzie and the other Williams Street for Hezekiah. Hayes City never made the list of top Texas towns, probably testimony to the fact that she should have never gone into a business venture with her husband.

Every fall Lizzie and Hezekiah went to St. Louis and conducted their business. From there, they traveled extensively over the United States. Out came the gorgeous silks, taffetas, and velvets that made up Lizzie's luxurious wardrobe. One year they went to New York, where the cattle queen bought diamonds then valued at about $10,000. Among her treasures was a pair of four-carat diamond earrings, a lavish tiara, and a sunburst pin with eighty-four diamonds. She often wore her jewels when she traveled and attended special affairs at home. For daytime Austin, however, Lizzie dressed for the nineteenth century office. Her look was plain and frumpy with her hair, *sans* curls, sternly parted in the center and drawn back in a knot. With Lizzie, business demanded a business look.

For a change of pace, the Williams decided to move for a while to Cuba, one of their favorite vacation spots. Beef was big business there as well, and as usual Lizzie turned a tidy profit. One unfortunate incident occurred while the couple lived there. Hezekiah was kidnapped by Cuban bandits and held for a $30,000 ransom. Lizzie promptly paid for her husband's safe release. Some people suspected that Hezekiah himself had hatched the plot to pay off yet another debt. If indeed he had planned his abduction, Lizzie probably saw through it. She had an uncanny knack for seeing true motivation, especially when it had to do with money. One influential banker found this out the hard way when he tried to woo her with gifts. The bottom line was his bank wanted Lizzie's account. It happened in Galveston when they returned home from Cuba. The story goes that the influential island banker eagerly greeted her with flowers and arranged for transportation to their hotel, where he footed the bill for rooms. The couple took the offers, but Lizzie's business went elsewhere. She just didn't like bankers.

As Lizzie loved feathers, it wasn't surprising that she returned to Austin with a parrot. The bird, whom she adored, was quite a talker and became her constant companion. Some people thought she loved her parrot more than any person. She just didn't have much patience for human frailty. When Hezekiah's health began to weaken and trips to Hot Springs didn't cure him, she carted him off to his sons. She did not have any respect for Hezekiah's children by his first marriage, so she probably felt they deserved the distraction. Hezekiah died in El Paso in 1914. He and Lizzie were married thirty-five years but fortunately never had children. Lizzie would have had little patience. When Hezekiah's body was brought back to Austin for burial, Lizzie bought him the best—a very expensive, six-hundred-dollar coffin. When she paid the funeral bill, she wrote a note to the undertaker: "I loved this old buzzard this much," she scrawled.

By this time Lizzie was over seventy years old and a millionaire miser. A strange quirk began to dominate Lizzie's personality as her financial holdings became her primary purpose for existence. A friendless old woman, she began to keep churches, schools, and even the University of Texas on a string. She always gave them hope that she would donate large sums to their cause. She never did. Her credit remained good from El Paso to Galveston, but her unorthodox way of paying off notes always raised the eyebrow of the town banker. Once when she was in her seventies, Lizzie entered a bank and asked for her note. She then took out a large, red bandanna handkerchief full of greenbacks and counted out payment in full of several thousand dollars.

Lizzie lost interest in her health and her appearance after Hezekiah died, but she remained true to her pocketbook. An old-timer, T.U. Taylor, told *Frontier Times* that the elderly Lizzie ate some of her meals at the Maverick Cafe and always ordered the same thing—a ten-cent bowl of vegetable soup with bread or crackers. One winter, when vegetables were hard to come by, the cafe owner raised the cost of the meal. Lizzie made a contract with the proprietor that her bowl would remain at ten cents, whatever the season.

Home was a dreadful hovel without heat and only miserable furniture. Mrs. John Shelton, Lizzie's niece, tells of a time when she went to take care of her aunt during a bout of illness. She put all the wood that lay by the hearth into the fireplace in an effort to warm the constant chill in the barren room. She hurried out to fetch more only to find just one stick burning on the fire. The others had been rescued from the flame and piled again by the stove. Other stories about firewood have plagued the memory of Lizzie Johnson. All the rooms in her Brueggerhoff Building were heated with wood stoves. Each tenant was issued the wood, stick by stick, with the wood pile remaining locked in a storeroom. Once Lizzie became furious because she claimed that several pieces had been pilfered. When her nephew-in-law went to investigate for her, he found about five-hundred sticks of wood piled high. Apparently, Lizzie kept a running tally of the pieces.

Near starvation, eccentric Lizzie finally had no choice but to live with her niece. As expected, the old lady was a very difficult guest. She slept all day and wandered the house all night, muttering, "This is the wrong street—the wrong street." Fascinated with electric lights, Lizzie made her niece, Mrs. Shelton, leave them on all night. To build up her aunt, Mrs. Shelton began preparing eggnogs for her. A rabid prohibitionist all of her life, Lizzie had no idea she was getting a shot of whiskey in her "custard" she learned to love so dearly. When Lizzie became difficult, Shelton wisely allowed her hand to slip when pouring in the booze.

Lizzie Johnson Williams died without a will on October 9, 1924, at the age of eighty-one. A treasure hunt commenced with Mrs. Shelton in command. In an old bookcase behind a boarded-up pane, she located hundreds of dollars in five-dollar bills. Scattered around the room in various hiding places were one-hundred-dollar greenbacks. The fabulous diamonds and emerald ring turned up missing. Finally, after a tedious search, the jewels, wrapped in a scorched cloth, were discovered in the basement of a building on Sixth Street in an unlocked box. Yet, in locked containers were feathers from the beloved parrot and dried flowers from Hezekiah's funeral wreath.

After her death Lizzie's land continued to make money. Oil was discovered on some of the "worthless" land she owned, but descendants had already sold it. If Lizzie had lived, she would have become one of Texas' first oil barons, a label she would have relished. This female financier was buried next to Hezekiah at Oakwood Cemetery in Austin. With the hidden money and various assets including the jewels finally found, the total value of her estate was $187,441.11, not bad for a Texas cattle queen. If only Lizzie could have taken it with her.

Bibliography

Books:

Abernethy, Francis Edward. *Legendary Ladies of Texas: Publications of the Texas Folklore Society Number XLIII.* Dallas: E-Heart Press, 1981.

Dooley, Claude and Betty Dooley. *Why Stop?* Houston: Texas Historical Commission; Gulf Publishing, 1978.

Fischer, Ernest G. *Robert Potter: Founder of the Texas Navy.* Gretna, LA: Pelican Publishing Company, 1976.

Frost, H. Gordon. *The Gentleman's Club: The Story of Prostitution in El Paso.* El Paso: Mangan Books, 1983.

Groneman, Bill. *Alamo Defenders: A Genealogy: The People and Their Words.* Austin: Eakin Press, 1990.

Harman, S. W. *Belle Starr: The Female Desperado.* Houston: Frontier Press of Texas, 1954.

Hendricks, Louie. *No Rules or Guidelines.* Amarillo: Cal Farley's Boys Ranch, 1981.

Hinton, Ted and Larry Grove. *Ambush: The Real Story of Bonnie and Clyde.* Austin: Shoal Creek Publishers, 1979.

Hunter, J. Marvin. *Heel-Fly Time in Texas: A Story of the Civil War Period.* Bandera: Frontier Times, 1936.

_____. *The Story of Lottie Deno: Her Life and Times.* Bandera: The 4 Hunters, Publishers, 1959.

Jones, Billy M. *Women in Texas.* Waco: Texian Press, 1977.

Kirkland, Elithe Hamilton. *Love Is a Wild Assault.* Bryan: Shearer Publishing, 1984.

McLeRoy, Sherrie S. *Mistress of Glen Eden: The Life and Times of Texas Pioneer Sophia Porter.* Sherman: The White Stone Publishing Group, 1990.

Parker, Emma Krause and Nellie Barrow Cowan. *Fugitives.* Dallas: Ranger Press, 1934.

Rascoe, Burton. *Belle Starr.* New York: Random House, 1941.

Richardson Rupert N. *Texas, the Lone Star State.* New York: Prentice Hall, 1943.

Rister, Carl Coke. *Fort Griffin on the Texas Frontier.* Norman: University of Oklahoma Press; Norman Publishing, 1956.

Robinson, Charles III. *The Frontier World of Fort Griffin.* Spokane: The Arthur H. Clark Company, 1992.

Russell, Traylor. *The Diamond Bessie Murder and the Rothschild Trials.* Waco: Texian Press, 1990.

Sandwich, Brian. *The Great Western: Legendary Lady of the Southwest.* El Paso: University of Texas at El Paso, 1991.

Steele, Phillip W. *Starr Tracks: Belle and Pearl Starr.* Gretna, LA: Pelican Publishing Company, 1989.

Tolbert, Frank X. *The Day of San Jacinto.* New York: McGraw-Hill Book Company, 1959.

Turner, Martha Anne. *The Yellow Rose of Texas: Her Saga and Her Song.* Austin: Shoal Creek Publishers, 1976.

Winegarten, Ruthe. *Texas Women: A Pictorial History.* Austin: Eakin Press, 1986.

Newspapers:
Dallas Morning News, 8 January 1933.
Dallas Morning News, 7 July 1963.
Dallas Morning News, 30 April 1989.
Ft. Smith Arkansas New Era, 22 February 1883.
Houston Chronicle, 22 July 1952.
Houston Chronicle, 26 June 1961.
Houston Chronicle, 27 June 1961
Houston Chronicle, 14 January 1962.

Houston Chronicle, 22 July 1962.
Houston Chronicle, 21 April 1984.
Houston Chronicle, 19 June 1986.
Houston Chronicle, 14 January 1991.
Houston Post, 23 October 1958.
Houston Post, 28 October 1958.
Houston Post, 26 June 1961.
Houston Post, 1 December 1985.
Houston Post, 21 January 1986.
Houston Post, 5 March 1991.
San Antonio Express News, 29 May 85.
Seguin Gazette, 3 January 1990.
Spirit Of The Times [New York], 25 July 1846.

Chapters or Parts of Books:

Blake, R.B. "Menken, Adah Isaacs." *The Handbook of Texas*. Austin: The Texas State Historical Association, 1952.

Frost, Gorden. "El Paso Madams." In *Legendary Ladies of Texas*, edited by Francis E. Abernethy. Dallas: Texas Folklore Society; E-Heart Press, 1981.

Gorzel, André and John Neal Phillips. "Tell Them I Don't Smoke Cigars: The Story of Bonnie Parker." In *Legendary Ladies of Texas*, edited by Francis E. Abernethy. Dallas: Texas Folklore Society; E-Heart Press, 1981.

Hunter, J. Marvin. "The Lottie Deno I Knew." *West Texas Historical Association Year Book*. Abilene: West Texas Historical Association (October 1947), 30-35.

Maguire, Jack. "Sophia Porter: Texas' Own Scarlett O'Hara." In *Legendary Ladies of Texas*, edited by Francis E. Abernethy. Dallas: Texas Folklore Society; E-Heart Press, 1981.

Kilgore, Dan. "Two Six-Shooters and a Sunbonnet: The Story of Sally Skull." In *Legendary Ladies of Texas*, edited by Francis E. Abernethy. Dallas: Texas Folklore Society; E-Heart Press, 1981.

Palmer, Pamela L. "Adah Isaacs Menken." In *Legendary Ladies of Texas*, edited by Francis E. Abernethy. Dallas: Texas Folklore Society; E-Heart Press, 1981.

Paulissen, Maisie. "Pardon Me, Governor Ferguson." In *Legendary Ladies of Texas*, edited by Francis E. Abernethy. Dallas: Texas Folklore Society; E-Heart Press, 1981.

Roberts, Emmett. "Frontier Experiences of Emmett Roberts of Nugent, Texas." *West Texas Historical Association Year Book*. Abeline: West Texas Historical Asociation (June 1927), 52-53.

Robertson P.D., and R.L. Robertson. "Mystery Woman of Old Tascosa." *Panhandle Pilgrimage*. Amarillo: Paramount Publishing Co., 1976.

Shelton, Emily J. "Lizzie E. Johnson: A Cattle Queen of Texas." In *Legendary Ladies of Texas*, edited by Francis E. Abernethy. Dallas: Texas Folklore Society; E-Heart Press, 1981.

Steen, R.W. "Ferguson, James Edward." *Handbook of Texas*. Austin: The Texas State Historical Association, 1952.

Syers, William E. "Griffin's Mystery Lady." In *Off the Beaten Trail*. Waco: Texian Press, 1992.

Jones, Billy M. "A Texas Cattle Queen: Lizzie Johnson Williams." In *Women in Texas*. Waco: Texian Press, 1977.

Jones, Billy M. "Miriam Amanda Ferguson." In *Women in Texas*. Waco: Texian Press, 1977.

Turner, Martha Anne. "Emily Morgan: Yellow Rose of Texas." In *Legendary Ladies of Texas*, edited by Francis E. Abernethy. Dallas: Texas Folklore Society; E-Heart Press, 1981.

Winegarten, Ruthe. "Belle Starr: The Bandit Queen of Dallas." In *Legendary Ladies of Texas*, edited by Francis E. Abernethy. Dallas: Texas Folklore Society; E-Heart Press, 1981.

Articles from Journals and Magazines:

Buchanan, A. Russell. "George Washington Trahern: Texan Cowboy Soldier from Mier to Buena Vista." *The Southwestern Historical Quarterly* (July 1954): No. 1, 60:19-22.

Henson, Margaret S. "She's the Real Thing." *Texas Highways* (April 1986): 61.

Hunter, J. Marvin. "The Mystery Woman at Ft. Concho." *Frontier Times* (January 1927) 1-3.

Lipscomb, Millie Gene. "The Saga of Lottie Deno." *The Junior Historian* Austin: Texas State Historical Association (December 1946), 7, No. 3, 1-2.

Norvell, James R. "The Ames Case Revisited." *The Southwestern Historical Quarterly*, No. 63 (July, 1959 to April, 1960).

Shelton, Emily Jones. "Lizzie E. Johnson: A Cattle Queen of Texas." *The Southwestern Historical Quarterly*, No. 50, (January, 1947): 349-366.

Thomas, Robert. "Lady Luck." *Ranch Magazine* (August 1983): 22-24.

Thonhoff, Robert H. "Taylor's Trail in Texas." *The Southwestern Historical Quarterly*, No. 70, (July 1966): 19-22.

Turner, Martha Anne. "Legend of the Yellow Rose." *Texas Highways* (April 1986): 58-61.

Tutt, Bob. "The Truth About the Yellow Rose." *Texas, Houston Chronicle Magazine* (2 February 1986): 5-6.

Wilson, Brian A. "Jim Ferguson and 'Ma': Turbulent Times for Texas." Texas, *Houston Chronicle Magazine* (November 2, 1986): 4-5.

Wood, Clement. "Ada Isaacs Menken: A Forgotten Deborah." *The Southern Magazine* (May 1924), 59-61.

Other Sources:

Bryan, J.P. Paper presented to Texas Historical Association, March 4, 1983. Text located in Battle of San Jacinto file. Daughters of the Republic of Texas Library at the Alamo.

Hunter, J. Marvin. "Lady Known as 'Maude' Beat Wild Life of Early Texas and Lived Down 'Past.'" Houston Public Library. Texas Biography, Texas Scrapbooks, 22A, p. 79.

West, Emily D. Research for text on Emily Morgan for *Handbook of Texas.* Houston Public Library. File on Emily Morgan. September 25, 1985.

Index